10 smart things gay men can do to improve their lives

Also by Joe Kort

10 Smart Things Gay Men Can Do To Find Real Love

Gay Affirmative Therapy for the Straight Clinician: The Essential Guide

Is My Husband Gay, Straight, or Bi?: A Guide for Women Concerned about Their Men

10 smart things gay men can do to improve their lives

Completely Revised and Updated Second Edition

joe kort

Smart Sex—Smart Love Books

Royal Oak, Michigan

Notice To Readers:

This book is intended as a reference volume only. It is not a
medical manual. The information contained in this book was
written to help readers make informed decisions about their sexual
practices and about health issues associated with sexuality. It was
not designed as a substitute for any treatment that may have been
prescribed by your personal physician. If you suspect that you have
a medical problem, see a competent physician to discuss your
concerns.

This is a revision of *10 Smart Things Gay Men Can Do To
Improve Their Lives* by Joe Kort, first published in 2003 by Alyson
Books.

ISBN 978-0-9973898-2-1

Credits:

"Everything Possible" Copyright © 1983 by Fred Small. Used by
permission. All rights reserved.

Cover Design by Hadrout Design

Contents

Preface

To The Revised and Updated Edition

It's been 13 years since the first edition of *10 Smart Things Gay Men Can Do To Improve Their Lives* was published. That doesn't seem like a long time, but a lot has happened. In 2003, there were no signs that gay marriage was ever going to be legal. The gay men that appeared on TV and in movies were just beginning to be more than caricatures, villains, or clowns. There were no gay apps or social media. Gay men still mostly chose to segregate themselves in their own bars, baths, community centers, and gayborhoods, and the straight people seemed to prefer it that way. A gay guy thought long and hard before coming out at work, at church, or (especially) at school.

The world has changed in many ways since 2003, and my thoughts and perspectives have evolved since then, too. I've revised *10 Smart Things Gay Men Can Do To Improve Their Lives* to better reflect what we're dealing with today.

Social Media

A big change in the way gay men socialize has been the apps like Grindr and Scruff and all the rest that make connecting so much easier than before. When this book was written in 2003, online dating was just getting started, and many people were still very suspicious of it. We were trying out chat rooms, but there was a stigma associated with meeting someone that way rather than in person.

In this revision, I've added case examples where men are using apps to meet, so that we can consider the positives and negatives of our new app-driven social scene.

The apps are especially good for shy men. Using an app, you can meet without being face-to-face, which is a boon for gay introverts, as well as the conflict avoidant and the guys a little too worried about their age or looks. The apps are an absolutely great way to approach people (and be approached) without having to worry about the kinds of things that come up in person.

Another benefit of social media in general is that it has encouraged us to open up more about our sexuality, what we like and what we don't. We were already talking about all that, of course, but the flood gates are now really open.

The apps are a versatile set of tools. They can be used for dating, for quick sex, or for finding friends. If you're looking for friends, you're going to find friends. If you want sex, you'll get sex. If you set your mind to finding a partner, you will discover other gay men who are looking for that, too.

A negative of the apps is that people can get hooked on them. An app can become an obsession for a guy. He's looking at it at work, looking at home, obsessed with finding the next man. Feeling out of control, he'll delete the app, and then re-install it the next day and keep looking. So, using gay apps really demands a lot more self-control than when you had to go out to meet men. The Internet gave us easy access; the apps give us even more. Some gay men come into my office, saying, "I'm addicted to this app. I can't stop. Help me!" They're not really "addicted." It's just new. It's exciting. It's a fantasy come true that you can have access to all these different bodies.

Straight men would have the same problem with control if there were a heterosexual Grindr. While straight people do have the app called Tinder, the difference is that women are not as easy to pick up and engage in hookups as men are. As I've said many times, this tendency to overdo sex is not a gay problem. It's a *guy* problem. It's not addiction. It's human nature. Still, it can be something that gets out of control and needs to be addressed.

The Way the Straight and Gay Communities Relate to Each Other

Since 2003, we have witnessed a phenomenal change in the way the straight and gay communities relate to each other. Put briefly, straight people are now mostly okay with us. There is still lots of discrimination, but there's so much more acceptance. Straight people are glad to have gay friends. They're empathic. They're compassionate to us.

Another difference these days is that gay men are not so self-segregating. They prefer to be in straight bars, amongst themselves but mixing with straight people. When I wrote this book in 2003, we had gay bars. We had gay cruises. Now the bars are closing down. A lot of the younger gay men don't want to be in a gay ghetto, a "gayborhood." They don't want to be segregated, and straight people as a rule are totally fine with that. Younger gay guys don't relate to the safety of having our own spaces the way we older gay guys did.

Gay Homophobia

However, one issue from 2003 is still with us. It stands out even more to me in the light of acceptance by the straight community. It is our own internalized homophobia. That was a core theme of this book originally, and it still is. We have trouble recognizing and accepting ourselves. We enjoy our gay friends but still put down "gay life." Straight people do that a lot less today than they did before.

After this book was first released, I went on a book tour and was surprised to discover how well *10 Smart Things Gay Men Can Do Improve Their Lives* was received in places like San Francisco, Chicago and New York. I knew it would have some popularity in the Detroit area because I was known locally, but I didn't expect it to have such resonance where gay life was out and open and free. The men at my book-signings explained: Even though they had moved to gay-friendly cities and could easily live "out and open" lives, they still had unresolved internalized homophobia. My book encouraged them to recognize and deal with their ongoing burden of self-hate and gay shame.

Sex Positive

I've changed since 2003 especially in that I have become more sex positive. Thirteen years ago, I was deeply influenced by the point-of-view of "sexual addiction." Since then, I've learned more about human sexuality. I've become a certified sex therapist and supervisor. And in this time period, I've treated many clients who were troubled by their sexuality, and I've seen time and again that they have not been helped by the sex-negative therapies and perspectives of the sexual-addiction industry. In that community, partnered, vanilla, heteronormative sex is considered the healthy ideal, and that stance is looking more and more naive and less and less helpful in the 21st Century.

So, the biggest change in the 2016 edition is that Chapter 5 no longer follows the precepts of sexual addiction. I no longer believe in that model or that label. It's overused, and it's used against people. When my clients are struggling with sexual issues, I want to look at their individual experiences and explore why they are problematic on a case-by-case basis. Most of the reasons turn out to have nothing to do with compulsivity or loss of control, even though it's often experienced that way. Most people with sexual problems can recover simply by having effective sex education. Not just basic sex education but education on the variations of sex and sexuality.

Today, we know so much more about sexual fluidity, kinks, fetishes, non-monogamy and all the rest. Sex is messy, smelly, gross at times, exhilarating, highly energizing and (often) fun. Sex cannot be perfectly integrated with our laws, principles, and ideals. "Most of us will get turned on at night by the very same things that we will demonstrate against during the day," as my colleague, Esther Perel, says so well. [1] Once people are educated about sex and understand what's healthy and what's not, they have a different perspective on what they're doing. The new Chapter 5 will help them understand that. The old Chapter 5, "Avoid or Overcome Sexual Addiction," has been replaced by "Explore Erotic Turn-ons and Sexual Interests." This change in titles alone illustrates clearly enough a transformation from sex-negative to healthy sex-positive thinking.

In fact, when I wrote this book in 2003, my perspective was *heteronormative.* I really did believe that the ideal gay relationship *had to be* monogamous, even though I understood (and research continues to show) that about 50 percent of stable gay relationships are open. Yet, I'm not the only gay man with heteronormative habits of mind. It's really puzzling to see gay men judge other gay men for *their* open relationships. Obviously, some of that comes from wanting straight people to accept us. But the truth is we're lucky we don't have to be just like them. We get to be free, and we're not free if we feel we have to model ourselves on straight people.

When I give talks, the individuals who seem to be most worried about open relationships are single gay men. They ask me, "How am I going to find a partner if 50 percent of gay men are in open relationships?" My answer is simple, "If 50 percent of gay men are in open relationships, then 50 percent aren't. That's a lot of men who are potential partners for you."

I'm not just more sex positive now. I've moved away from thinking any particular way of being sexual is more healthy than any another. Sexual fetishes, like variations on BDSM, used to be very controversial. The sex-addiction community labeled fetishes "addictions" that clients had to be "cured" of. But as Doug Braun-Harvey and Michael Vigarito state in their book, *Out of Control Sexual Behaviors: Rethinking Sex Addiction,*[2] healing compulsive behaviors should not be about giving oneself an erotic-ectomy! Now, BDSM is mainstream for both gay and straight, at least for the young people. And I no longer see it as automatically a problem.

Some people do need help with their "out-of-control sexual behaviors." (I prefer this less pejorative phrase to "sexual addiction.") However, a person can be very interested in sex and porn without being addicted. I used to imagine that I saw a great deal of sex addiction in the gay community. That was because I was seeing through my sex-addiction-trained sex-negative lenses. Now, I see that gay men have a lot of fun with sex and a lot more permission and a lot more opportunity, and I see all that through a much more positive set of lenses. I see it as healthier than I did back in 2003. My change in perspective is reflected in this revision of *10 Smart Things Gay Men Can Do To Improve Their Lives.*

One factor that has encouraged more playful and creative sexual expression in the gay community is that AIDS is less the inexorable death sentence it once was. That is partly unfortunate. There's less AIDS awareness now than there used to be, and so we're seeing an increase of men in their 20s contracting HIV. I've added a section to Chapter 5 reminding of the continuing importance of safe sex, despite progress in AIDS prevention and treatment.

It's ironic to note that today straight people are looking sexually more and more like gay people. They're having more open relationships. The whole BDSM thing is now mainstream, whereas it used to be considered dark and abusive, a figment of the underworld of "sexual deviants." (This change of attitude is illustrated by the mainstream popularity of the book *Shades of Grey*.) Oral and anal sex—now in the repertoire of most straight young couples—were illegal almost everywhere until recently because they were associated with "homosexuality." And yes, straight men have gone to prison for going down on their wives, as recently as 25 years ago.[3] Needless to say, gay people have been in the avant-garde of sexual openness and adventuring, variations and porn. It's the straight world that has changed around sex; they're catching up with us.

Honesty with Yourself

The way I see it now, your bottom line should not be a particular behavior, a particular mode of behavior, a particular choice in the way that you express your sexuality. You don't have to be monogamous. You don't have to be afraid of fetishes. You don't have to do *this*. You don't have to avoid *that*. Just be honest with yourself about yourself. Your job is to examine your own sexuality and get comfortable with what's right for you. I don't come from a place of pasting labels and making moral judgments anymore. What's your own sexual identity? Really. I mean that. "Your own," not what anybody tells you it should be. In particular, be very wary of any therapist who insists on telling you what is right or wrong for you regarding consensual sexual behaviors.

As you learn what you want and as you begin to try to focus on your goals, you may discover that "something" is holding you back. You keep trying, but you never seem to get any closer to where you want to be. I've helped clients with this problem many times in my office. Unresolved childhood issues affect almost every human being and can get in the way when you're trying to make things better for yourself. Childhood pain can carry over to adulthood through the unconscious mind, and be recycled in the present. I have had clients say to me, "I am not looking for a therapist to keep me in the past. The past is over. I am looking to be in the present and to go forward." The problem (I tell them) is that if they keep recycling the unresolved past into the present, they will be stuck in their old patterns forever. Only psychotherapy with an experienced therapist can get the resulting unresolved childhood blocks out of the way, so that these mysterious obstacles no longer undermine you. As I discuss in the revised Chapter 7, you will need the help of a psychotherapist, because negotiating by yourself with your unconscious mind is an almost impossible task. This has not changed since 2003 or 1903. Deal with your unconscious, or it will rule you.

Growing up gay generates extra unconscious obstacles that don't exist for non-LGBT children. These special unresolved issues need to be examined with a trained gay-affirmative therapist who understands what comes up for an adult who was once an LGBT child.[4]

Honoring Your Own Goals

Even though I end this book in Chapter 10 with a detailed description of my marriage, that's not any sort of ideal that I'm proposing. A committed monogamous relationship is good, if that's what you want. In 2003, I chose to end the book that way because I come from a generation when a stable gay marriage was hardly possible, and I wanted to say at that time that it was possible. Now, if you read this book and decide that's not what you want, that's okay. If you're a guy who wants to be single and have all kinds of relationships, then that's fine, too.

Discover who you are and honor what you discover. My example shows that one gay man can get what he wants even if it seems difficult, even if it seems *impossible*. When I discovered I wanted a monogamous relationship with a stable partner, I focused on men who would date with that in mind. Even though hookups are fun for everyone, and were fun for me for a while, I focused on serious dating and I put forward a rule of "no sex for three months." It was not always easy to hold that line, especially when a nice man I was dating didn't get it and refused to go along with it. He might have been a good partner for me, but I had my boundaries, and they were not right for him. We both had to move on. The point is I could hold my line because I knew myself and I knew what I wanted.

You can get what you want if you can focus with a serious mindset: First to know yourself—and be willing to suffer the pain of self-honesty—and then put aside distractions as you go for what is important to you.

Mentors and the Gay Community

When I wrote the book in 2003, I was in my late 30s. I sought out older gay men to teach me what it was to be a gay man. Now that I'm in my 50's, I've discovered that I am one of those older gay men, and I'm happy to mentor younger men. At the same time, I look to them to help me keep up with what it is to be a young contemporary gay man in our modern culture.

I love our gay community. I love mentoring young men. I loved being mentored when I was young. I still love being mentored. I didn't see all sides in 2003. It is this vision of gay community that I hope everyone who reads my book will discover and be delighted by.

But in one way society has not progressed since 2003. Gay children and teens still have no one to mentor them. Growing up gay is still a very isolating and annihilating experience for too many young people. While you are a gay little boy, our society—in its classrooms, its playgrounds, its religious institutions—has no place for you and doesn't want you to exist. You are erased. A gay little boy doesn't know who he can turn to, doesn't know who to trust. He hears people whispering, he watches TV, and he realizes how unsafe the world can be if you don't fit in. When he's older, when he can come out, then the world of 2016 really is different from 2003, and certainly from the 1980s when I came out. But gay children also need mentors, and right now that's not allowed.

The theme and purpose of this book is to improve lives. You can't re-live your childhood, but you can go forward and make your life better. You can take responsibility for your own life. If you're old enough to read this book, you can come out. You can follow the ten "smart things" presented here to find your way to the life you choose. Good luck, and let me know on my website www.joekort.com how you're doing.

References

1. Esther Perel, "The Secret to Desire in a Long-term Relationship," TED talk, posted Feb 2013.
2. Douglas Braun-Harvey and Michael Vigorito. *Treating Out of Control Sexual Behavior: Rethinking Sex Addiction.* New York: Springer, 2015.
3. Tina Dupuy, "Legalized: Oral Sex, Sodomy and Immoral Prosecutions," Huffington Post, 09/21/2009, updated 5/25/2011.

4. Joe Kort. *Gay Affirmative Therapy for the Straight Clinician: The Essential Guide*. New York: W. W. Norton & Company, 2008.

Introduction

What Works? And What Doesn't?

Alan was a 34-year-old consultant for one of the car companies in Detroit. He came to see me after experiencing depression over his gayness and his relationship with his partner of five years. He'd been seeing a heterosexual male therapist in town but felt he wasn't getting anywhere—either with accepting his homosexuality or resolving the conflicts in his relationship. His therapist referred him to me, telling him that I was gay as well.

Alan was handsome with boyish looks and tightly cropped hair. His trim body suggested that he was involved with sports, and in fact he did play soccer and baseball on a regular basis. For his first session, he came to my office dressed in his work attire—tie, white shirt, and wingtip shoes.

"Look at me!" he said. "I don't look gay. You don't. either. Maybe we're fooling ourselves. This is just wrong. This isn't how I envisioned my life. I wanted to be straight with a wife and kids by now."

Alan filled me in. Six years before, he had been engaged to a woman—then broke up with her. Secretly, he'd promised himself that if their relationship didn't work out, he'd act on his gay feelings and come out of the closet. He didn't want to make any other woman suffer with his inability to commit to her. He knew why he could not commit—he was gay. He could have sex with women, but he found it unfulfilling.

On the other hand, Alan didn't like being gay. He felt that he was giving into urges he was meant to repress. He was horrified at the idea of being out and open, with others—particularly his family—knowing he was gay.

Alan came from a small rural town in Michigan, where his family still lived in the house he grew up in. Hardly anything ever changed there. The furniture was the same as when he had been a child. Appliances from his childhood, aside from ones that absolutely had to be replaced, were still in use. It was as if time had stood still. His parents had the same jobs they'd held their whole adult lives, and they still spent every weekend at the local pub they'd always frequented. Alan recalled a few occasions in his childhood when his parents had taken him and his siblings along to the pub and left them in the smoky pinball game room, while the adults went to the bar to drink and socialize.

His macho, sports-oriented father worked a blue-collar job. At night, his mother worked on the line for one of the Big Three automakers. After school, they left Alan to fend for himself and take care of his younger brother and sister. When his father came home, he would sit on the couch, drink his beer, read the paper, watch television, and go to bed, never interacting with Alan or the other children.

With his mother at work, his father ignoring him, and his younger brother going off with friends, Alan felt neglected. He developed a special relationship with his younger sister, toward whom he still felt paternal. Their parents didn't make much money, so Alan stepped in to pay for her college education and sent her spending money as well. Their relationship was more father-daughter than brother-sister.

Alan couldn't conceive of admitting to his parents that he was gay. "That will never happen," he told me. "They would die. I can't do this to them. And my sister would lose all faith in me and have no one to count on. I can't let her down."

Soon after Alan came out at a local gay bar, he met his partner, Matthew. Alan had done little dating before Matthew. Being with him had been fun and exciting at first, but after their second year together, Alan felt unhappy because their relationship was "in a rut." Alan wanted more from Matthew; in particular, he wanted them to live together. Matthew agreed but whenever it came time for either of them to move in with the other, or to sell both houses and buy a new one together, Matthew came up with some reason why it wouldn't work. This had gone on for the three years before Alan came to see me.

Alan was angry at Matthew for not wanting to spend more time together. They saw each other once during the week and once over the weekend. Matthew claimed that with Alan in his bed, he couldn't get a good night sleep and couldn't function well at work. When he resisted making any move or changing his behavior, Alan would lash out. They would argue, and Alan would become enraged, shout, and slam doors.

He complained to me that Detroit was "a difficult place to be openly gay." Alan had no close gay friends, nor was he at all involved in Detroit's gay community. He thought life would be easier where there was a larger concentration of gay men. His only friend was a woman. They'd been best friends for over ten years, and she knew he was gay. He said he'd never come out to the men on his sports teams, because he felt ashamed and feared their judgment.

Alan admitted that part of his problem was that he didn't want people to know he was gay. If he went out to dinner with a male coworker, he didn't feel people were staring, but if he and Matthew went to dinner, then Alan was sure everyone would know they were gay—much to his embarrassment.

Alan complained about Matthew's being "stuck in a rut," but Alan was stuck, too—with a large amount of internalized homophobia. He blamed his difficulties on being closeted in society and living in Michigan, and he blamed Matthew for not participating more actively in their relationship.

In our work together, I tried to help Alan focus on his childhood, because he seemed to be replaying exactly what had happened to him then, back when his parents neglected him through work and alcohol. Now he found himself with a partner who, he felt, was neglecting him. His frustration with Matthew was understandable, but his high level of anger was an overreaction. It belonged to his relationship with his parents.

He said that my making the connection to his childhood made logical sense, but he wasn't feeling any angry or hurt emotions toward his parents. "They did the best they could, and I don't want to blame them for anything."

No matter how much work Alan did, in both individual and group therapy, he couldn't reach his true feelings about his parents. He came to my workshops to help gay men heal and rid themselves of self-hatred and homophobia. He went to gay events in the community, but he still felt bad about being gay. He stayed closeted at work and to the guys on his sporting teams. His relationship with Matthew stayed the same, even though many times Alan threatened to end it.

Finally, though, it was Matthew who broke off with Alan. One night at Matthew's house, Alan became so angry, he threw something across the room and broke a window. Matthew told him he'd had enough and ended the relationship.

Now Alan found himself in a bind. Not feeling any progress, he'd dropped out of the gay men's group the year before. He had no network to support him. His symptoms of depression grew worse. He couldn't tell his family what was going on. He had no one to talk to but me.

Isolated and alone, Alan was back where he had been as a child, but he continued to deny that his childhood was at all related to his current situation, or that his overreaction to Matthew's distancing in their relationship was really a replay of how he'd felt as a child.

I didn't think Alan could make much progress until he came out more, and I told him so. I felt that he'd find, stored away in his closet, many other feelings and memories about his childhood. But he wasn't ready to deal with it all. I expressed concern that he'd keep feeling isolated, lonely, and abandoned—unless he addressed the issues of his parents' neglecting him when he was a child.

Again and again, I see clients make the same mistakes. And inevitably, I find myself giving exactly the same advice over and over. Reading this book, I hope you'll recognize the stumbling blocks, both internal and external, that have held you back from living an effective, totally fulfilled gay life. Each of these ten smart things is a solution to a specific problem that clients have brought to my office time and again.

Over the years, I've seen what works and what doesn't. Now I'd like to make these "prescriptions" available in book form for every gay man to use.

These ten smart things are kind of a checklist—answers to the challenges any gay man may face, at one time or another, throughout his life. None of these chapters is a cookie-cutter, one-size-fits-all prescription, but each contains important insights. Throughout, I'll give you real-life examples based on my work with clients who put these basic principles to work in their own way—almost always with considerable success and satisfaction.

I ask every one of my clients (and everyone who reads this book) to recognize that he's a unique individual. Health and happiness are your birthrights. And, yes, you happen to be gay. So to live a rewarding life as a gay man, you must tailor anybody's advice—mine included—to fit your own particular goals and circumstances, always keeping your own values, lifestyle, and personal strengths in mind.

In the upcoming chapters, I'll introduce you to gay men who've crippled themselves emotionally (and often sabotaged their romantic relationships as well) by not coming out to anyone except themselves, their partners, and a few close friends. In most cases, their self-protective impulse only serves to keep them isolated. You'll also meet heterosexually married men who, in their 40s and 50s, come out of denial and admit they've been gay all along. They experience a profound sense of liberation when they find the courage to come out, being honest with themselves and their families.

You'll read how coming out to your family can reawaken—even worsen—the dysfunctional problems that have lain dormant in the closet. But you'll also learn how men from 15 to 75 have forged deeper, warmer bonds with their parents, siblings, former in-laws, even their children.

I'll explain why gay men are so often criticized for being "childish" or "immature," and how to avoid falling victim to gay culture's overemphasis on looks, youth, and glamour. Afraid of growing old? I'll offer you numerous remedies, including meaningful involvement in your local gay community, serving as a mentor, and giving other gay men (both younger and older) the benefits of your own hard-won experience.

I will explore with you the specific ways in which problematic sexual behaviors manifest in the gay male community. Often, sexual issues are rooted in psychological issues and will respond to a combination of individual and group therapy. You'll learn why so-called reparative therapies—to "cure" our homosexuality—can't possibly work. At the same time, you'll learn about the genuinely helpful "therapy workout" opportunities available to every gay man. Is the best therapist for you male or female, gay or straight? Stay tuned!

Perhaps most importantly, I'll show you how to keep your romantic relationship with another man alive and evolving as you both pass beyond the first stages of infatuation, through the inevitable power struggle, and on to deep and abiding love.

Believe it or not, your most serious quarrels and disagreements are potentially healthy, and can lead to tremendous personal growth for you both, as partners and individuals.

Even if a wedding doesn't feel appropriate for the two of you, you'll want to read about other gay couples who have taken that courageous step—with all the frustrations, surprises, and joys that went with it.

You don't need to be a Mensa member to do smart things and to start reaping the benefits. Hundreds of my clients have already proven to my satisfaction (and, more importantly, to their own) that these choices *work*.

Psychology can seem dauntingly complex, and sometimes a bit scary. Might there be some things lurking down in your subconscious you'd rather not hear about? No need for timidity. I will work to keep things as clear, accessible, and practical as I can. My clients—from their early teens to their 70s, from every walk of life—help dramatize the issues and hassles that every gay man must (and should) face. Armed with their wisdom, clarity, and understanding, you can keep on making personal breakthroughs while enjoying the special advantages that gay culture has to offer.

You need not agree with every word I say. While reading about the dozens of gay men who have come to me for help, however, you're sure to recognize many of the challenges you're facing right now.

Every one of the ten smart things has the same goal: To help you live *happily, confidently*, and *successfully* as a gay man— inside and outside the gay community.

Chapter 1

Take Responsibility for Your Own Life

It is hard to love yourself more than you have been loved.

—author unknown

True: It's hard to love yourself more than you have been loved. But while it is difficult, it's not impossible. Let's see how you can love and empower yourself as a gay man.

Nick and his partner Rolf had been together for five years and had just relocated from California. They came to see me because one year earlier, Nick had logged onto their shared computer and found emails from other men, some with nude pictures attached. When confronted, Rolf admitted that up to that point in their relationship, he'd secretly had sex with many other men. Ever since, the two had struggled to get back to a safe, trusting relationship.

Rolf claimed that since his original confession, he'd had sex with no one but Nick. He was adamant: "I've done nothing!" But Nick was still distrustful and didn't believe him.

Nick stated that Rolf's behavior only reinforced what he already believed about the gay community: Monogamy is a joke and a myth. All gay men are promiscuous and have lousy moral values. Nick was angry and disappointed that "gay life has to be this way." He remained with Rolf only because, as he confessed, "I don't believe it's any better out there with those guys who parade in drag or in leather, and give gay men a bad name."

Nick simply wanted Rolf "fixed." He wasn't willing to look at his own role in their relationship problems. Dutifully, Rolf started to attend my therapy group for men struggling with out-of-control sexual behavior (OCSB).

In our work, I pointed out that promiscuity and infidelity aren't unique to the gay male community. They're a *male* issue, not a gay issue. Scan the tabloid headlines at the supermarket checkout, and you'll see that cheating and promiscuity are challenges for straight men, too. Nick had bought the commonplace stereotype that many ignorant people preach: We gay men are sexual beings only and nothing more. (Very often, what looks like promiscuity is really a symptom of postponed adolescence—more about that in Chapter 4.)

Very often, OCSB results from sexual abuse in early childhood. Therapy can help survivors of this kind of abuse, and Rolf was getting it. But Nick wasn't willing to explore how his own past contributed to the problems in their relationship. In fact, his childhood was traumatic. His parents had abandoned him, leaving him to be raised apart from his siblings by an aunt and uncle. Despite this obvious source of suffering, Nick felt that Rolf's behavior was all they needed to address.

Even though Nick denied it, I suspected that it wasn't really Rolf, but his own parents whom Nick wanted to condemn for not staying committed and being there for him. In Chapter 9, I explore why we choose partners who remind us of familiar, beloved caretakers from our childhood—and what happens as a result. In this instance, Nick was projecting—transferring onto Rolf his negative feelings and beliefs about his family and gay life in general.

In the end, Rolf continued to work on his own issues, but Nick left him, without ever resolving their situation. Predictably, Nick met other partners who fit his assumption that gay men couldn't be monogamous and committed to him. Because of his unwillingness to look at himself and to resolve his own personal issues, he never learned differently.

You Can Fix Only Yourself

An ancient Chinese proverb states that a long journey starts with a single step. The point, of course, is that determination is the key to any endeavor. Without that do-it-yourself resolve to *make* things happen (as opposed to *waiting around* for them to happen), any attempt at a successful life—gay or otherwise—is doomed from the get-go.

Very often, my clients begin therapy by talking about how society marginalizes us gay men and forces us into being sex junkies. They complain that they can't do anything about it, because gay male culture supports sexual promiscuity. I remind them that heterosexists and homophobes do marginalize us. And, yes, there's a strong emphasis on sex in our community, but there's nothing wrong with that. Gay individuals can still decide what they will do and not do sexually. (In Chapter 5, you'll discover how to deal with aspects of your sexuality that have been troublesome to you.)

Gay men entering my office also know that I'm a certified Imago Relationship Therapist (see Chapter 9). Often, like Nick, they want me to help them figure out what's wrong with their partners, who need to change. Instead, we talk about what their partners might say about *them* and the troubles that their partners might be having with *them*. When each partner takes responsibility and vows not to point his finger at the other, only then can we begin to examine what contributes to problems in the relationship,

Trying to fix another person is a dead-end road. More important—and far more effective—is to make the effort to clean up your side of the curb. Once clients are able to do that, they can realistically examine whether their relationships can survive. Luckily (as you'll see in Chapter 9), they often can.

The 12-step Serenity Prayer goes: "Grant me the serenity to accept the things I cannot change, the courage to change the things I can, and the wisdom to know the difference." Over the years, some people have modified it as follows: "Grant me the serenity to accept the people I cannot change, the courage to change the only person I can change, and the wisdom to know who that person is—me."

In my practice, I see a lot of gay men who don't get this. Until they recognize who that person is, true change remains beyond their reach.

Other clients complain that the gay community is "superficial," "cliquey," "picky," or "judgmental." After further conversation, it's apparent they're voicing more of their own internalized homophobia. In the next chapter, you'll meet one of them, Carl. Once Carl identified the negative lens he used to see the world, his issues with our gay community were greatly reduced. Feeling better about being gay, he started to let go of many of the judgments he'd held about other gay men. He realized his prejudices simply reflected how he felt—or more exactly, how he had been taught to feel—about being gay.

Yes, some of the judgments of men like Carl are based on reality, but learning how to create your own reality is the real challenge.

Is It Society's Fault?

Other men begin our conversation by trying to explain why they didn't come out of the closet earlier in life. They hold society responsible: "That was the 1950s [or the 60s], and no way could I have been out back then." But that doesn't explain why so many other gay men felt safe enough to come out during those times. As you'll see in the next chapter, a man can have many reasons not to come out that may be just as important, if not more important, than the fear of social stigma.

Often, a gay man is (unconsciously) aware that if he does come out of the closet, he'll have to deal with other psychological "dust bunnies" that he has swept under the rug—issues like finding his authentic self and dealing with family traumas and issues.

Clients like Nick criticize the gay community, and sometimes make homophobic remarks about Gay Pride events: "Why do *we* have to have a parade? Straight people don't need parades." I respond by asking, "Do you feel the same way about the St. Patrick's Day Parade, or the Jewish Walk for Israel, or the various ethnic festivals we have here in Detroit?"

They usually say, "No," adding, "But that's different. Those festivities aren't about sexuality." Nor are Gay Pridefests. Yes, some of the men dress in drag or leather, but don't marchers in the Irish parades and ethnic festivals also wear their ethnic "drag"?

There's a whole culture for gay men to celebrate, honor, and witness just as these other events and festivities do, but many of us see through a negative filter imprinted early in childhood.

Don't Hate Who You Are

Internalized homophobia is very common. Again, this process is unconscious; we're not aware of it. From infancy, we're handed messages that being gay is "wrong" and "bad." So many gay men believe the myths and lies perpetuated by heterosexuals—and by gays as well.

Then one day—usually in our early teens—we discover that our true, authentic nature is the very thing we've been taught to loathe. We take the homophobia that's been drummed into us and direct it inward, toward ourselves. Again and again in my office, I see the harm and destruction that result when gay men can't accept who they are and—worse yet—judge themselves and others by heterosexual standards. This internalized homophobia often compels gay men to be cruel to themselves and each other.

Psychology 101 teaches the concepts of projection and transference. *Projection* means assigning your own characteristics to other parties in your life. It can be both positive and negative. We constantly make up stories—often, total fantasies—about other people's thoughts, motivations, and intentions. Only rarely do we stop for verification, or give others a chance to tell us who they really are. We think we know a person, and there it ends. Problem is, our story is often more about us than about the other person.

Back when I was taking an Imago Relationship training course for therapists, I was shocked to hear a woman who, after 30 years of marriage, was just beginning to discover who her husband really was. Until then, she'd been making up stories about her spouse— few of them accurate. She'd assumed that her unspoken opinions and judgments corresponded to his feelings and experiences.

Her stories about him were really about her. Whenever she felt down in the dumps, she believed that he didn't respect her "moods" and couldn't tolerate her depressions. Not so. He was simply trying to cheer her up and help her feel better, always with the best of intentions. Her projections arose from her belief that if he really loved her, he'd respond to her in certain ways. This is "magical thinking"—the belief that others will know what we want, without our telling them. It was the woman's responsibility to tell her husband that she needed to work through her depression on her own. We consider this further in Chapter 9.

Being Outraged Is Usually Overreacting

We're born into a culture that generally encourages negative projections toward gay men. Tell some heterosexuals that you're gay, and they automatically imagine you in bed with another man and then accuse you of pushing your sexuality in their face. But this is projection: They're blaming you for "making" them imagine your sexual behavior.

A school principal once invited me to give a presentation on homosexuality to a group of teachers in his school system. They knew I was coming and understood the topic I was going to present. Afterward, I learned that some teachers had been so upset they'd stopped listening—or even walked out—simply because I talked about my partner. They felt it was "inappropriate" for me to talk about my "personal" life, and that I'd been "preachy" to talk about him and to stick my "gayness" in their face. All I'd done was refer to Mike, naturally and honestly, as an important part of my life as a gay man. If a heterosexual male referred to his wife or girlfriend, people would not get up and leave the room. They'd never accuse the speaker of pushing his sex life in their faces.

Judgments are an inescapable part of daily life. But for gay men, judgment often spells danger, since we're usually judged unworthy as soon as we reveal who we really are. The accumulative effect of these negative judgments takes a toll on our lives. But at the same time, they can contain valuable insights that we shouldn't overlook.

I agree with the client who told me, "Our Creator gave us two ears and one mouth, so we can listen twice as much as we talk." This concept is easy to grasp, but hard to put into practice. It demands that you stop pointing your finger at other parties and ask what your reactions—especially when they're out of proportion to the situation—say about you.

If you react strongly to people who behave in certain ways or say certain things, your reaction says more about you than about those to whom you're reacting. In fact, about 90 percent of any exaggerated reaction is about yourself.

Big reactions are appropriate for phenomena like gay-bashing, the Holocaust, child molestation, and serial killers. However if someone cuts you off in traffic and you give him the finger, your response is out of proportion to the situation. Maybe the driver didn't see you or really didn't mean to cut you off. Irritation is appropriate. Being outraged and even vengeful is overreacting.

Projections, Transference, Judgments, and Shadows

Transference means taking the positive and negative traits of significant, influential people in our lives and unconsciously transferring them onto somebody else—usually, one's partner, friend, colleague, or therapist. It commonly happens with the people we feel closest to. We professionals actually hope for this. We want clients to transfer their feelings onto us, so we can help them see the issues they have with other people in their lives, resolve them, and move on.

Imago Relationship Therapists understand that this phenomenon is normal in relationships. We try to help couples understand that partners do engage in transference with one another and that it's usually a positive indicator they're in a healthy relationship.

No one is free from projection, transference, or judgments. The crucial issue is to learn how to deal with them. Judgments are not innately "bad." You can use them in very effective ways once you accept that your reactions are your own and that they tell you a lot more about yourself than about the people you judge.

Our LGBTQ culture is under constant assault. Virtually every day, some newspaper article or TV program takes issue with somebody who's openly, visibly gay. The Boy Scouts have allowed us in their troops only grudgingly and under pressure, and the same is true for the armed forces. Many churches won't allow us in their pulpits.

What's the best way to stand up to bigotry? Every gay man who reads this book should resolve to stop feeling like a victim and to become an empowered adult. Yes, societal problems do exist. We all have to combat insults, offenses, and tragedies. But, first, start to work on yourself, as an individual. Only after you determine the psychological effects of cultural abuse can you lay those issues to rest and move ahead with your life.

Only then can you be an effective activist on behalf of our LGBTQ brothers and sisters.

Psychologist Carl G. Jung coined the term "Shadow" to describe the parts of the one's self that are repressed, undeveloped, or denied. He taught that if we are in shadow, we project denied aspects of ourselves onto others. Inner dynamics "in shadow" are ones you're not consciously aware of, but which nonetheless run at full speed.

Contrary to popular belief, your Shadow can be positive as well as negative. Yes, if repressed, it can cause considerable damage. But as soon as you recognize and accept it, it can be a source of tremendous psychological wealth.

Robert Bly, a respected poet, is best known for his ground-breaking men's movement best-seller, *Iron John*. In his later book, *A Little Book on the Human Shadow*, he discusses how projections bleed away your personal energy.[1] In other words, when you ascribe your own best qualities and character traits to others, you deny and deplete them in yourself. I couldn't agree more. The very traits you strongly dislike – or like, for that matter—in others (including straight society) usually reflect some unresolved issue lurking inside you.

For example, if you idealize another person and therefore overreact to them, you may overlook positive aspects of that person reflected in you. Similarly, if you focus on hating others' behavior or character traits, you won't have the knowledge to deal with those same defects in yourself.

We diminish ourselves by staying in Shadow. Whenever a client overreacts to some "outside" issue in his life, I see it as a signal that he's really talking about himself, in some not-so-indirect way.

In 1992, I wanted to advertise my gay men's group therapy and weekend workshops. I created a mailing list of addresses just by thumbing through phonebooks and scanning for local gay listings and gay-friendly businesses. I printed up a batch of one-page flyers, tri-folded them, and affixed a sticker to make sure they'd stay shut. I added a stamp, my return address, a forwarding request, and dumped them in a mailbox. I figured that if the recipients weren't interested in my flyer, they would simply toss it or pass it along to a friend.

By then, I had been openly gay for 12 years. I'd grown quite distant from the kind of homophobia I was about to face. Following the mailing, I received several heartening calls from men in the Detroit area, eager to join a gay men's group. But other callers were outraged, asking, "How dare you send me this mailing about a gay group with no envelope?" If they were closeted, they might have feared their child, husband, or wife would see my flyer and connect the dots. Others were simply annoyed at my presumption that they were gay. Would they have been offended if I presumed they were straight?

Every year I receive thousands of letters about Attention Deficit Disorder, menopause, diabetes, and rape. I never worry how these senders single me out. I never take offense, but lots of others do—if they get mail dealing with LGBTQ subject matter.

Most of those who overreact this way are in their own shadows. My mailings (now emailings) simply inflame their own inner conflicts. I determined not to let homophobic reactions stop me from providing—and promoting—effective, supportive therapy to our LGBTQ community.

I hope that while reading this book, you'll identify your own projections, transference, shadows, and judgments. Reclaim the good in yourself that you've been overlooking or giving away. Increasing your self-awareness and taking responsibility for your own life are the only (certainly the fastest) ways to achieve personal freedom as a gay man. Becoming accountable for your own words and actions is what integrity and responsibility are all about. If you remain focused on what other people do and say—or won't do or say —that means asking them to be responsible and accountable for your own happiness. Surrendering your own welfare into their hands will only leave you angry and empty, a hostage to what others want—or expect you to be.

References

1. Robert Bly. *A Little Book on the Human Shadow*. New York: HarperCollins Publishers, 1988.

Chapter 2

Affirm Yourself by Coming Out

It is better to be hated for who you are, than to be loved for who you are not.

—Andre Gide

The first step to living a full life—coming out of the closet—is no small task. Women can be very close friends, enjoy deeply meaningful relationships, and say "I love you" to each other without anyone thinking they are lesbians. But when men talk about being best friends and attend social events together, people suspect they're romantically and sexually involved.

When he sees teachers, parents, and other authority figures practice homophobia and heterosexism, the gay young boy learns to hide. Actually, hiding can be a smart move on his part, because being out—in the wrong place at an inappropriate time—can mean ostracism, abuse, and even physical and psychological injury. Gay male teens often have to pretend to be something they're not. They must make many decisions, consciously and unconsciously, about how to deal with their homosexuality.

In my many years as a psychotherapist, I've met many gay men who were shamed into hiding their orientation and pretending a sexual interest in—even marrying—women. Some honestly did not know they were gay. Their intentions were honorable. They hoped their homosexual "leanings" would somehow just "go away."

Ironically, when these men can no longer live their lives in hiding, conservative people blame *them* for coming out and ask, "If you knew you were gay, why did you marry a woman in the first place? How could you do this to your wife and kids?"

Love Is the First Awakening

Beginning the coming-out process triggers many different life events. Generally, when a woman has sex with another women, she begins to consider the possibility that she's a lesbian. Society permits a woman to love other women openly and affectionately, but it's taboo for her to be sexual with another woman, unless she's performing for a straight man's entertainment and arousal.

By contrast, men often have sex with other men and never label their experience homosexuality. Instead, they can keep it secret and deny it. They may seek men online, hire an escort, or have a self-identified gay man service them orally—and then forget about it, so they don't have to deal with their difficult feelings. Not until they fall in love with another man do they begin to consider they might be gay. Powerful emotions like love are just harder to deny.

Victor, a successful 25-year-old car salesman with a wife and a set of pre-school-aged twins, came to therapy because he'd discovered he was gay. Until recently, he reported, the thought of being gay had never entered his mind. He'd had close male friends and never questioned his feelings for them. He'd never had any sexual encounters with them, though he'd had some sexual fantasies of being with other men. But he just figured everyone had them and decided not to give them too much thought. He was happily married and loved being a husband and father—until he went on a sales trip in a neighboring state.

On the plane, the man in the next seat struck up a conversation. Unsure at first what was happening, Vic found himself sexually attracted and thought the feeling was mutual. When they landed, Andy gave Vic his card and told him what hotel he was in. After checking in, Vic couldn't get his mind off Andy. He went through his normal business day but that evening found himself compelled to call. Over dinner, Andy admitted that he was gay and wanted to have sex with Vic, who couldn't believe his ears. For the first time in his life, he began to wonder if he were gay. He was strongly attracted to Andy in many ways—not just sexually.

That night, he accepted Andy's invitation. Never had Vic had a sexual experience so good, right, and exciting. After the trip he returned home, riddled with guilt.

Cheating was not part of his value system. Yet he felt a call from deep inside himself, separate from his marriage. Vic and Andy kept in touch and found they had lots in common. Vic was falling in love with Andy. Andy eventually joined him on another business trip. After their week together, Vic knew, without doubt, that he was in love—and that he was gay.

His tension, guilt, and emotional devastation were overwhelming. What would he do? His twins had just turned three. What about his marriage? Though divorce wasn't part of his value system, it tortured him to be dishonest. Vic decided to come out of the closet. These details, his attorney warned, could only work against visitation rights.

His wife, parents, and in-laws were enraged. All of them asked him the same question: How could he marry, knowing he was gay? No one believed his assertion that he hadn't known. Once Andy walked into his life, Vic confessed, the floodgates opened, confirming his real identity.

Vic's wife tried to use his homosexuality as grounds to deny him contact with their toddlers. The judge dismissed her motion. Not all gay men are so lucky.

Repression and Suppression
Vic and the other men I've treated have actually not been bisexual. When I ask, they tell me that women don't excite them sexually. They could perform sexually with their wives because they loved them. But no other women caught their gaze. In the

well-known prison syndrome, inmates have sex with other men—even fall in love with them—but they aren't bisexual. Upon their release, they return to strict heterosexual behavior, because that's their orientation.

It takes gay men a while to discover themselves. Even so, boys tend to discover they're gay earlier than girls. Some of my clients report they knew as early as age 3 that they had homosexual feelings, but didn't know what to call them.

A boy quickly discovers what's acceptable and what's not. If he tries to dress up Barbies, touch another boy, or play house, he swiftly realizes his impulses and desires are unacceptable. He is usually shamed into stopping the behavior. Girls are given some leeway to play with boys' toys and to join in their sports. They're allowed to have sleepovers and brush each other's hair.

Not all gay boys care to play with girls' toys. In fact, some straight boys do. But the boy drawn to "sissy" behavior learns that something is "different and wrong" with him. During this period of introspection, he discovers his gayness earlier than his lesbian peer.

My heterosexual sister didn't like wearing dresses, and she identified with boys. We have a snapshot of her playing baseball, holding a bat, and wearing a uniform. We all laugh and say how cute she looked during her tomboy years. For her, it was a stage she grew out of.

In "Tomboys and Cowgirls: The Girl's Disidentification from the Mother," Dianne Elise says, "A tomboy becomes a short-lived, insignificant phase that we ignore or humor out of existence as merely a lapse in the ongoing stream of feminine development."[1] Why, then, do we make such an issue out of sissy boys?

When I was young, I'd put my sister's black tights on my head, wear one of my mother's dresses, pretend I was Cher, and lip-sync to her music. I assure you, there are no family snapshots of little Joey's sissy years. That was a stage for me, too.

There is no acceptable time period for a young boy to explore his feminine side, because his exploration would call attention to the fact that he might be different. Boys cannot touch each other unless the contact is sports-related, so *wanting* to touch another boy is another red flag. The tendency to break cultural taboos doesn't necessarily indicate a young male's sexual orientation, but it definitely calls for him to become introspective—and to realize that he is different—at an earlier age.

Many clients report "sissy-type" histories similar to mine. Nonconformity to gender role expectations doesn't create homosexual orientation, but it is a positive indicator for a gay boy's later development. Similarly, the smothering-mother/absent-father combination doesn't *make* a boy gay, but it is a common parental *reaction* to a son's being gay.

Such experiences force young gay boys into the closet. This means abandoning essential parts of ourselves to conform to social conventions. We repress (an unconscious process) and suppress (consciously) sexual impulses and fantasies. As we mature, we avoid other men who might be gay.

Carl, 31 years old, came to me because he had trouble finding a relationship. He'd been out for 10 years to his friends and family, but couldn't find a partner. He attributed this to his poor self-esteem and he believed he "wasn't attractive enough for the gay community."

While exploring his history, it became clear that all the friends to whom he was out were straight. He had no close gay friends at all. Carl was attracted only to younger guys around 20. His pursuits always ended in heartbreak. Young men of that age are emotionally and developmentally different from men of 31.

I immediately identified his internalized homophobia: He had no supportive gay male friendships because he believed that gay men are all promiscuous,

Carl didn't like being labeled homophobic. On his second visit, he told me he was angry and almost hadn't returned. Over the course of therapy, he saw how some of his actions and thinking were in fact internalized homophobia. Not until he came out of the closet could he have faced this issue.

He began to attend my workshops for gay men, where we examine the impact of internalized homophobia. Carl became more comfortable about his gayness and, while going for his Ph.D. degree, came out to his peers and teachers—something he'd never have done before. He felt much better as an openly gay man and began to talk about leaving therapy. But certain things still bothered him.

He soon realized why he was so attracted to young men of 20. They were around the age Carl had been when he dropped out of college to avoid pursuing a full gay life. He had suffered for 11 years. On his awakening, he was still 20 years old emotionally.

Faking It as a Heterosexual

When gay men are taught to display a false public self and to hide their true feelings, they enter a socialization process all children go through. In a family where parents admonish their son, "Don't be angry," a boy learns to hide his anger or finds other ways to express it. If a student learns what's appropriate to win social acceptance, he'll conform. We call this peer pressure, to which only "geeks" and "nerds" who are socially "out of it" are immune. But LGBTQ individuals have an additional task—to publicly display heterosexuality. Their core sexual and romantic identity is buried, along with the other traits necessary to build social skills.

In *Keeping the Love You Find: A Guide for Singles*, Harville Hendrix speaks about the social journey we all must take to develop our sense of self.[2] We're born with most of our thinking, feeling, and sensory functions intact. In a healthy family, parents send messages that it's okay to be you, to experience all of your body senses, to have feelings and express them, to solve problems, to be assertive. But that's not always what happens. Instead, we often get conflicting messages.

The messages we accept—or choose to obey—help to determine our place in the family we grow up in—even the culture we live in. Hendrix says that people develop a "fugitive self" that goes underground, where even heterosexuals sometimes have to hide. Because we want our parents and primary caretakers to return our love, we decide—in our childhood brilliance—to lose those potentially troublemaking aspects of ourselves and to pretend they aren't there. Of course, they're not really gone for good, but they're certainly out of our conscious scrutiny. I use Hendrix's ideas in my workshops to emphasize how gay men's core sexual identity gets buried along with any other "unacceptable" and "unfashionable" traits.

Like Carl, all of us develop a lost or denied self. In essence, a person hides who he really is and presents a false self to the world. Eventually, he believes the lie himself.

In a fortunately rare medical disorder, the afflicted cannot experience physical pain in their limbs. Nerve receptors that are meant to send physical-distress messages to the brain cease to function properly. Wouldn't it be nice to be forever relieved of aches and pains? No! Horrified parents find afflicted children finger-painting in their own blood, or a man steps on a nail which scratches the bone and he does not feel it until infection sets in and the limb needs to be removed. We *need* pain to avoid injury and as a signal that we need medical attention.

You see the parallel: The lost and denied self cannot "feel" whatever threatens it—and by extension, the individual as a whole—until it's too late. First, we consciously suppress these parts of ourselves as foreign to us. Then we *un*consciously repress them—so that they become literally "out of sight."

For example: A mother warns her daughter, "Don't act too smart, or boys won't be attracted to you." That girl grows up not believing herself intelligent, when of course she is.

Similarly, a boy who is told not to sit or stand or walk in certain ways loses touch with his own body. The boy becomes the gay man who's clueless about his urges.

The aspects of personality "lost," denied, and suppressed are different for everyone. Lost for all closeted gay men, however, is the possibility of romantic and sexual relationships. "The longer you stay inside your closet," I remind clients, "the more it transforms into a coffin, where only death exists. There's no room to grow."

To disguise their authentic selves, gay men spend enormous amounts of time throwing others off the track. This destructive expenditure of energy can lead to panic disorders, erectile difficulty, drug and alcohol abuse, a total shutdown of libido, OCSB, even suicide attempts.

At least 30 percent of teenagers who attempt suicide do so because they are struggling with their sexual identity. Where childhood sexual abuse is a factor, and when the perpetrator is the same gender as the victim, the boy wonders, "Am I gay or straight? Did I make that happen?"

Harry, a 34-year-old single office manager, complained of a lack of sexual or romantic desire. He had no desire for either gender. The very thought of being sexual at all—even masturbation—caused him nausea and extreme psychological discomfort. His primary care physician had ruled out any medical disorder.

Harry had never thought of himself as gay or straight, had never had a romantic love relationship, and had been sexual with only a few men and women. He enjoyed both, but found himself bothered by—and ashamed of—his gay encounters. Harry constantly worried that others might think he was gay. Moreover, he was also HIV-phobic. He refused to have gay roommates. He was afraid that people would label him gay if his roommate was gay, and he was afraid that he would contract AIDS from them in nonsexual ways.

In our work, Harry discovered that he was avoiding others, sexually and socially, to avoid addressing his core orientation. He agreed to attend one of my men's therapy groups. Harry's isolation made it hard for him to get close to other group members—participants said they "felt a distance" from him.

In the group, Harry became increasingly uncomfortable. He also attended my workshops, where he identified himself as bisexual. Repeatedly he objected to the workshops' structure, the seating arrangements, and the hours involved. Later, in therapy, he agreed that these trivial complaints were simply outlets for his discomfort at being with other gay men. All weekend long, he worried that someone he knew would see him entering the building where the workshop was taking place.

After six months of both group and individual work, Harry chose not to continue to try to resolve his sexual orientation. He confessed that he was most comfortable being alone and that therapy only made him more anxious. At this time, he wasn't ready or willing to do more. As a group, we all honored his decision. Men deserve the right to find their own way at their own pace.

Coming All the Way Out

I often tell the following joke at my workshops: A man asks a tailor to make him a suit. After being measured, he leaves and returns a week later—to find that one sleeve of the jacket is too short. The tailor tells him, "Bend your arm and raise your shoulder. Now it fits perfectly."

"But the other sleeve's too long."

Again, the tailor suggests that he bend and raise his arm. The sleeve fits perfectly. "What about the pants?" the client asks. "One leg's longer than the other."

The tailor shows him how to adjust his legs up and down until the suit fits perfectly. He's now twisted like a pretzel—but his suit fits like a glove. He pays the tailor and walks off down the street.

Two women see him hobbling. One says, "What a wonderful tailor, to make a fine suit for such a physically disabled man!"

We gay men are told to put on a suit that doesn't fit us, and we gamely try to pretend that it does. Others call us "crippled," so we begin to think we really are. But there's nothing wrong *with* us: What's wrong is what's been done *to* us. We need to take off the psychological suits that others have assigned us and begin to see ourselves without shame. And we need to find another tailor!

How do we do this? By coming out.

Many of my clients decide to be out in various—usually limited—ways. Some are out only to themselves and to me. Much of this reticence is justified: As media stories of gay-bashings attest, coming out in the wrong place at the wrong time can have grave consequences. But in places where men may come out without putting at risk their jobs or physical safety, learning to live outside the closet is essential.

Many gay men I've worked with say they want to come out, but they don't think it's necessary to tell everyone what they do sexually. "Other people don't need to know about my sex life," they often say. I point out that being gay isn't just about sexuality. Even if a gay man were celibate, he'd still be gay.

If a man's going to come out, he must recognize that his act isn't an *admission* of what he does sexually but an *affirmation* of who he is romantically, spiritually, emotionally, and psychologically.

Some clients don't feel the need to come out to their family or friends. "They already know," some say. I challenge them: "Then what's the risk in telling?" Even if these people *do* know, why not be open? Often clients say they don't need to tell, because "Straight people don't tell me they're straight." I reply that straight people don't have to out themselves formally. They are already out.

Heterosexism assumes that everyone is straight until proven otherwise. Straight people talk openly about their spouses, their girlfriends and boyfriends, and the singles bars they frequent. If a gay client omits this kind of information, I usually suspect internalized homophobia.

Many clients say, "I'm waiting for Mr. Right. Then I'll have a reason to come out." I reply, "Why aren't *you* Mr. Right-Enough? What can waiting for another man possibly do for you?" We explore how this is a rationalization, a psychological defense to postpone coming out. What's more, this strategy reduces a client's chances of ever finding a partner.

Gays who desire to be partnered before coming out often want to emulate the heterosexual world, where being half of a couple is valued more than being single. For many gay men, being single is yet another blow to their self-esteem. When Rosie O'Donnell came out on *Prime Time*, Diane Sawyer asked, "Why come out now?" Rosie replied, "I wanted to wait until I was in a long-term committed relationship." Many gays and lesbians feel more empowered under these conditions.

What can gay men expect when they begin the coming-out process? Vivienne C. Cass's model of *homosexuality identity formation*[3] best reflects my own process of coming out and the stages I've observed in my clients. There are six stages: 1. Identity Confusion, 2. Identity Comparison, 3. Identity Tolerance, 4. Identity Acceptance 5. Identity Pride, and 6. Identity Synthesis.

Stage One: Identity Confusion

According to Cass, the first step is *coming out to yourself.* During this stage, a man begins to notice, recognize, and acknowledge his own sexual attraction to other men. He might not see himself even remotely as gay; he still identifies as heterosexual. This isn't role-playing—he honestly believes he is straight.

In my years of practice, I've met many clients who worry they may be gay, because they have same-sex fantasies or even encounters. But merely wondering whether one is gay or having sexual contact with another man is not necessarily Stage One of coming out. There are a number of things to rule in and to rule out. The fantasy or behavior might be a manifestation of childhood sexual abuse by a male perpetrator. Or it could be motivated by the sexual thrill of breaking a taboo, in this case the homosexual taboo. Some bisexual or bi-attractional tendencies have nothing to do with one's core sexual identity. This is discussed in more detail in my book, *Is My Husband Gay, Straight, or Bi?*[4]

This is the stage where many psychotherapists can do harm. Most don't even know about the stages of coming out. Many try to reassure their clients by offering all kinds of explanations for homosexual behavior. They often overlook the possibility that their client is beginning the process of self-recognition that will reveal his gay identity. I think it's important to go further and inform clients that homosexual sex can mean a lot of things—as well as the possibility that they're at Stage One of the coming-out process. But because this causes so much discomfort for many men, some therapists' good intentions (and, often, their own homophobia) prompt them to steer clients—particularly male adolescents—away from such thoughts.

Many therapists have told me they're reluctant to educate a teen about homosexuality for fear that he'll become excessively upset or wonder why his therapist is bringing this up. They usually report to me that in their attempt not to overload a client—teen or otherwise—they "let those thoughts go their own course" and don't fully explore them. Some well-meaning therapists don't explore them at all and even avoid the client's expressions of same-sex desires.

I think this kind of avoidance is harmful in itself. I usually tell a client, "There are a number of possibilities here." If the man's struggling with his feelings for men, I don't push the word *gay*, because I believe it's an affirmative word that defines an entire way of life—including romantic, spiritual, psychological, and sexual connection to other men. Many men have homosexual desires but are strictly "hetero-emotional." Although they are sexually attracted to men, they are romantically interested in women only.

After I have taken a thorough history of the client's background and educated him about the stages of coming out, the client can then make his own decision. It's arrogant for us therapists to decide for a client who he is or isn't, or who he should or shouldn't be.

Also, during this undecided first stage, men begin to consider going for reparative therapies that propose to "cure" homosexuality. Men who pursue this option do a lot of damage to their self-esteem and consequently to their lives. I ask clients to consider that there's nothing to cure. They might decide not to act on their homosexual desires or ever to come out—that's their decision. In my therapeutic judgment, homosexual feelings don't need to be "cured" or "repaired."

Stage Two: Identity Comparison

During this stage, a man begins to accept the possibility that he might be homosexual. Again, he would not use the word gay, because of its association with a particular way of life. *Homosexual* is simply a word he can use to start exploring sexual feelings from a "safe" distance.

In Stage Two of the coming out process, men begin to feel positive about being different. They might also accept their *behavior* as homosexual, while they still reject homosexuality as their core identity. Finally, they might accept their identity, but inhibit their homosexual or gay behavior—by deciding to marry a woman or by having anonymous "no strings" sex, for example.

It's here, I believe, that psychotherapists—LGBTQ therapists in particular—do damage by forcing the issue. After exploring homosexuality, some people may decide it's not for them. Their decision isn't a product of shame or guilt. These clients don't see homosexuality as something that needs to be cured or fixed. Instead, they simply discover they're not connecting to a gay identity. Just like adults who, having been raised Jewish or Catholic, decide to change religions, they must decide on the identity that fits them best.

Yes, I realize I'm treading on thin ice. Many would accuse me of helping people live a life fraught with depression which, according to the American Psychological Association, is the usual fate of those who live a closeted life. I agree with the APA, but as a Gay Affirmative Psychotherapist, it's my job to help clients feel good about their homosexual feelings and gay identity. And to help people become who *they* want to be, not who I think they should be.

If a client committed to reparative therapy asked to see me, I'd tell him that this therapy is abusive and refer him elsewhere. However, I have supported some men who decided for themselves that a homosexual identity wasn't for them and planned to enter a heterosexual marriage. My coaching here usually involves educating them about life in the closet and about the APA's warnings. To help them make an informed choice, I fully explain that they need not feel wrong or bad for having these feelings. That is where we should ground any important life decision. I also coach these men to be forthcoming to any women they might become involved with.

Darryl, 36 years old, came to me depressed about his job situation. His company had just been bought out, and his new boss had increased his workload. He had been heterosexually married, with no children, for nearly 14 years and loved his wife deeply. At his workplace, he told his Employee Assistance Personnel (EAP) counselor about his homosexual feelings. Knowing that I specialized in issues involving homosexuality, she referred him to me.

Darryl stated he'd "acted out" homosexually during his late teens—before meeting his current wife—and reported feeling a lot of shame about it. Over the years, he'd worked with many different therapists, who all informed him that his feelings were rooted in his unsatisfying relationship with his father. According to these therapists, Darryl had sexualized his desire for a strong father figure. In his primarily heterosexual therapy groups, these therapists told him to keep his homosexual feelings to himself, lest he suffer negative feedback and judgments from his peers within the group.

Darryl complied. He didn't share much with his therapists because they simply told him, "If you don't give your feelings much energy, they will go away." They never did, of course, and Darryl was ashamed of this part of himself and saw it as a pathology.

Before making the referral, his EAP had already told Darryl I was gay. When I asked if that was a problem, Darryl's said, "No. Maybe looking at this from a gay person's point of view for a change might help."

During our work together, Darryl was finally able to talk at length about his sexuality. He told me he could have enjoyable and satisfying sexual relations with his wife. He was able to be 100 percent fully engaged with her and didn't think about men or other women. (Many self-identified gay men confess they have to think of men while having intercourse with a woman.) Darryl did say that other women didn't excite him in the least. He was always sexually drawn to men and had had all of his other sexual experiences with men.

Darryl felt his homosexual impulses were something to be ashamed of and indicated that he was "less of a man." His parents would often compare him unfavorably to other males. Darryl was convinced this had led to his homosexual feelings—and his previous therapists supported his conclusion. While I can see how this experience could lead a client to eroticize males, I didn't think this was true for Darryl. He was sexually drawn to men and not at all to women. Again, his romantic attraction to his wife led to a sexual arousal and positive experience. In other words, while Daryl was not sexually attracted to women, his wife could sexually satisfy him because he was romantically connected to her.

Significantly, women often report that this is true for them as well: They're attracted to a man romantically and their sexual feelings are secondary. They often state they need romance in order to feel sexual.

Darryl could never imagine being in a relationship with another man. Unable to be romantic with men, he'd be unfulfilled in any gay relationship. He was "shocked" to learn I had been with my partner for so long (at that time, about six years) and even more shocked to learn I planned to marry him. He often told me he thought I was "playing house" and only "kidding myself" when I said I had a good life.

This is an example of negative transference; Because Darryl didn't believe he could have a fulfilling gay life, he pushed his negative beliefs about homosexuality onto me.

He entered a Men's Sexuality Group I facilitated that included gay, bisexual, and straight men. For the first time, Darryl heard gay men speak about loving, caring, intimate relationships in a positive, healthy light. Still, he felt that his own sexual feelings for men reflected his low self-esteem. He didn't identify himself as gay and interpreted his homoeroticism as a form of pathology.

Over five years of therapy with me, both individually and in group, his negative feelings about his homosexuality lessened. Eventually, he told his wife that I, his therapist, was gay. I thought this might be a prelude to his finally telling her about himself. He reported that she was tolerant and accepting of gay men when he raised the topic, but he didn't believe that she would be okay with his having the same impulses.

Darryl had never acted on those impulses during his marriage. What a tribute to his wife that he remained faithful! Many group members praised him for being faithful and showing integrity, but he couldn't take that in. To accept it would mean honoring himself as a man, which went against the messages his parents had given him—that he was not a "real man."

I believe it's important for partners to be able to tell their significant others who they are, so I coached Darryl to consider telling his wife about his sexual feelings for men. Otherwise, he was hiding an important part of himself. He resisted telling her because he didn't want to leave her, to be sexual with men, or to "come out." None of that fit him. He worried she'd think that he wanted out of the marriage or that he would leave her after his confession.

Darryl agreed to attend my gay men's workshop and threw himself into the exercises. After completing the entire weekend and returning to group therapy, he began self-identifying as bisexual. He grew more comfortable with his sexual feelings for men.

Finally, he decided to tell his wife. His effort at honesty was a success. Although shocked, his wife honored his bravery and his commitment to their marriage. His depression lifted, his self-esteem improved, and his therapy was complete.

Darryl, I believe, is both hetero-emotional and homosexual. I think that if homophobic therapists hadn't told him that his feelings stemmed from an eroticized father figure – and if he had had a more positive exposure to gay culture—Darryl might have realized that he was okay and accepted his homosexual feelings earlier. In any case, what's important is that he's living the life *he* wants to live. He needed to remove the stigma from his feelings for men and claim his birthright to have complex sexual feelings.

Unfortunately, during the second stage, many gay men choose to seek reparative therapies. The negativity these therapies attach to being gay only further shames a man into believing his condition is "wrong." Reparative therapists don't offer a balanced approach to help men make educated, self-affirming decisions. It's simply not healthy to devalue one's gayness, which poses serious consequences to one's self-esteem and mental health.

Stage Three: Identity Tolerance

Here, the individual accepts the likelihood that he is homosexual and begins to move toward using the word *gay* to describe himself. (This isn't the case for those who decide not to continue their coming-out process. While Darryl was in Stage Two, he did not identify himself as being gay.) At Stage Three, the client begins to consider a homosexual identity—trying it on to see whether it fits. He may still hesitate to venture into the gay culture. Bad experiences might push him to decide that although he accepts himself as gay, he doesn't want to live openly as gay.

Ahmed was a 24-year-old chef's apprentice, living at home with his widowed Algerian mother. He was very self-conscious about his dark skin and premature hair loss. He had identified himself as gay for some time, but he was having bad experiences as he tried to enter the gay community. Men at gay bars were judgmental about his heavy Algerian accent. Some men he approached even told him that his hair loss made him unattractive.

Another factor that brought Ahmed to treatment was his family's opposition to his being gay. Generally, in Islamic cultures, it's not safe to be out.

Ahmed had met many other Arabic men who were closeted and who would not socialize with other gay men outside of all-gay functions. This consistent denial turned Ahmed off other Arabic men and gay life. In the gay community, on social media, and in his family, all of his experiences had been negative. As a last

Notes...

resort, he decided to enter therapy with me. "If this doesn't work," he confessed, "I might closet myself for the rest of my life."

In Ahmed's view, the gay community was superficial and overly sexual, and the straight community was unaccepting and hostile. The Talmud has a wise saying: "We see the world as we are, not as it is." Ahmed viewed everything from his own, limited perspective.

There is no one gay or straight community. Each community has many facets. You can find what you are looking for, but you must persevere. That was the essence of my coaching with Ahmed—to help him find the right places for him. For starters, I told him the bars and gay apps (like Grindr, Scruff, and others) were out.

Straight or gay, bars and apps are usually where people are looking for Mr. Right Now, not Mr. Right. Generally speaking, the bar scene is one big high school—developmentally and emotionally, everyone's about 16 years old. That isn't to say bars don't have their time and place. I prompt many of my clients to go to bars socially for a good time. They meet someone? Fine. A few men have met lifetime partners at bars, but I coach them not to expect this.

Ahmed came to my gay men's workshops. As a "good son," Ahmed found the parts of the workshop relating to family very difficult. The hardest part for him was fear of letting his family down. He knew they would never fully approve of him, would have to go through a grieving process, and would have to admit they were the mother and siblings of a gay son and brother— something not acceptable in their culture. He made strong friendships at the workshop and even dated some of the men after the weekend. His self-esteem went up, and these positive experiences helped move Ahmed toward an affirmative acceptance of his gay self.

Returning to the gay community center, he found more people with whom he could relate. Yes, some men there still judged him for his "baldness and heavy accent." But he was able to overlook this and approach men who weren't judgmental. Ahmed then moved toward the next stage of coming out.

Stage Four: Identity Acceptance

This is the movement from simple tolerance to accepting—and identifying—oneself as gay. Now the individual discovers a new sense of belonging, seeking how to fit into the gay community as a whole. He feels increasing anger at the anti-gay segments of society—and this is healthy, too. He takes all the doubt and self-hatred he used to direct inward and diverts it outward at more deserving targets.

Again, as a healthy reaction, he distances himself from people and places that would disrupt his new way of thinking and his new self-acceptance. This is very similar to the adolescent male who, having gone through puberty, starts identifying with his growing sexuality. And, just as teenagers experience an acute need for privacy, he distances himself from his family. He keeps his door closed, adopts music and fashions (which he knows his parents won't like) to set himself apart from them, and bonds with his peers, who recognize his newfound sexual self. Few parents are delighted when a teenager goes through this stage, but school counselors and therapists normalize this process. It's a passing stage, necessary for the teen to get a sense of belonging and forge a personal identity.

This is appropriate—nothing to worry about. Similarly, Gay Affirmative Psychotherapy sees identity acceptance as normal for individuals of any age. Like an adolescent accepting his new identity, a gay man may well choose new friends and hangouts to shield himself from any negative views about his homosexuality—or anyone else's. Gay Affirmative Psychotherapy honors this stage as developmentally appropriate. See my book *Gay Affirmative Therapy for the Straight Clinician.*[5]

Stage Five: Identity Pride

The next stage even more closely parallels the stages of adolescent development. Here, the individual totally accepts his own self-image, even as he becomes equally aware of society's rejection of it. To bridge this dilemma, the gay man will reinforce, even emphasize, the differences between being gay and being straight. A teenager might dye his hair blue, pierce his body, and horrify his parents with "outrageous" behavior. The gay man might plaster his car with rainbow stickers, vacation in San Francisco or Key West, and out himself to everyone in his life.

All his previous repression is now explosively directed outward. This is when he wants to be interviewed on *Ellen* and come out to the world. He'll read only gay literature, devouring all the aspects and trademarks of gay culture. He starts to disdain the heterosexual world—now it's "them against us."

This stage creates the best activists. His combination of anger and pride spark the gay man to become heavily, passionately involved in gay rights organizations and Gay Pride marches. On the downside, this is where this same man might be judged as "too" gay. (In 1997, Ellen DeGeneres decided to come out— personally and in character—on her hit television show *Ellen*. The remainder of the series was an illustration of identity pride, centering for the most part, on gay issues. Even gay people accused both Ellen and *Ellen* of being "too gay.")

It's important to recognize Identity Pride. In my office, I often see middle-aged men wearing T-shirts that say, "I CAN'T EVEN *THINK* STRAIGHT," sporting Gay Pride rainbow hats, or driving to my office in a rainbow-plastered car.

They often proclaim that they're gay and proud, even if they feel a little foolish acting out in this manner at their age. They don't yet fully understand their own behavior. Also, there's tremendous grief inside them—they wish they'd made this change earlier in life and sometimes mistake their behavior for a "midlife" crisis. I reframe it for them as a life-awakening and educate them on the stages of coming out. I reassure them that they're just in the "gay adolescent" stage of Identity Pride—a necessary step for their self-actualization as gay men. Almost always, they breathe a sigh of relief when they learn there's a name for their experience.

Clients are sometimes afraid to achieve this stage—or afraid they'll get stuck in it. "I don't want to become a gay man and wave a rainbow flag around." While I reassure them that doesn't have to happen, I also explore their possible homophobia: What's wrong with a little flamboyance?

When I returned home from the 1993 Gay Pride March on Washington, many gay friends—and clients—were angry that the television news media focused mostly on the "drag queens, leather queens, and rainbow waving activists."

"Did you go?" I'd ask.

"I wouldn't be caught dead there," was the usual response.

Many clients are frustrated that heterosexual society focuses only on gay sexual and flamboyant behavior, not on gay men who lead ordinary lives. Still, those in-your-face gays and activists were brave enough to get out there and fight for the rest of us.

The final stage of the coming-out process is:

Stage Six: Identity Synthesis

At this stage of integration, the concept of "them and us" is no longer useful. The gay man begins to understand that not all heterosexuals are anti-gay. Like an older adolescent, he can relax his militant stance and reintegrate himself with the whole of society. He understands that heterosexism and homophobia exist, and that there's a power imbalance in the world, but this state of affairs does not dominate his life. He can relate both to gays and to straights without losing his self-confidence.

Coming out is a lifelong journey; it never ends. Cass's six stages describe a step-by-step process, but every man is different. Clients veer back and forth through all the stages. Some men come out to more and more people, at different stages of their lives. When I first came out to myself, I looked up the word "homosexual" in library books and all the textbooks we used in high school. Then, during my teen years, I came out all over again to therapists. I came out to my family, then to my friends in college. But I didn't come out professionally until I was well into my 20s. Each new day provides a fresh chance to progress in this journey.

References

1. Dianne Elise. "Tomboys and Cowgirls: The Girl's Disidentification from the Mother" in *Sissies and Tomboys: Gender Nonconformity and Homosexual Childhood,* Matthew Rottnek, ed. New York University Press, 1999, 150.
2. Harville Hendrix, Ph.D. *Keeping the Love You Find: A Guide for Singles*. New York: Owl Books; Reprint edition, 2001.
3. Vivienne Cass. "Homosexual Identity Formation: A Theoretical Model," in *Journal of Homosexuality*, Vol. 4 (3), 1979, 219-235.
4. Joe Kort with Alexander Morgan. *Is My Husband Gay, Straight, or Bi?: A Guide for Women Concerned about Their Men*. Lanham, Maryland: Rowman & Littlefield Publishers, 2014.
5. Joe Kort. *Gay Affirmative Therapy for the Straight Clinician: The Essential Guide*. New York: W. W. Norton & Company, 2008.

Chapter 3

Resolve Issues with Your Family

A man can't make a place for himself in the sun if he keeps taking refuge under the family tree

—Helen Keller

Of all the relationships in your life, family ties are usually the most intense and tightly organized. Most people want to stay connected to their families. There's comfort there, a feeling of safety, with people you've known virtually forever. They usually command the strongest loyalties.

But all too often, once you tell your family that you are gay, suddenly you're an outsider in your own family. Imagine your fear of introducing something so unexpected, perhaps so despised, that you might lose their support and respect. The prospect is chilling.

At age 42, Paul was a successful radiologist. Attractive and friendly, he came to me for help in coming out. He didn't want to threaten his "close knit" family by disclosing that he was gay. In our work together, he was able to see that he'd been closeted for so long to avoid revealing his secret to potentially hostile family members. He hadn't befriended or dated gay men or entered the gay community in any way. What if a friend or relative recognized him and outed him to his family? He dreamed of moving out of state to make it easier to come out and to avoid "burdening" his family.

He began to recognize that by not telling them, he'd sacrificed a lot. Because he had distanced himself so as not to be "discovered," his family relationships had become superficial. He worried that if his sister learned he was gay she'd forbid him contact with his young nephews, whom he adored.

Paul had deep, repressed resentments toward his family. He thought they knew he was gay. "It would be so much easier if they would just ask. Then I could simply answer, 'Yes.'"

We talked about his need to take the necessary steps. Whether they suspected Paul was gay wasn't the issue. He had to take the lead.

Our work together focused on his getting the courage and finding the words to tell them. Only after doing so would it be possible for Paul to move on with his life. And as his therapy progressed, he knew this more and more surely.

When he finally did tell, his mother and siblings were all relieved. They'd all suspected but dared not ask for fear that he wasn't ready to talk. They trusted that he'd tell them when he was ready. Relieved, Paul could now begin to move on with his life, enter the gay community, and not worry that he would run into anyone who would tell on him.

Heart-To-Heart Talk

Yes, an openly gay man risks being rejected by his family, but, paradoxically, by *not* talking, the gay man is rejecting them. LGBTQ individuals usually want to tell their families, but understandably they are scared. However, the very act of telling demonstrates their strong commitment to staying connected.

At age 18, I told my parents I was gay—one of the most frightening things I've ever done. This was 1981, and I had no role models, nobody to tell me how to proceed. At that time, all the therapists and psychological literature claimed that boys became gay because of how they were raised. It was all my parents' fault. When I told them, I feared I might lose everything.

Earlier, at age 15, I'd tried to tell my mother. I was on the expressway with my beginning driver's permit; she was in the passenger seat. It was a bright and joyous time: the Chanukah season. But my timing wasn't ideal, and my presentation even worse.

I started to weep, saying I had "something awful to tell her" and trying to explain how I was "different." I couldn't go on. She touched my shoulder and told me that everything would be fine. Later, she gave me some Chanukah money and placed me in therapy.

The first therapist called my gayness a "pathology." In his words, "You were meant to be heterosexual, as everyone is. But based on how you were raised, your sexuality has become distorted. I think you could go either way, and heterosexuality is the more normative, easier route." Despite his wrong-headed view of gayness, at least he provided me with a safe place to talk. He had me describe at length my feelings, fantasies, and dreams. I became increasingly comfortable talking about my homosexuality, and that helped as I was coming out.

I needed that, but I needed more. I needed to be applauded for the courage to talk about my gay self. Straight teens receive that applause whenever they have a heart-to-heart with mom or dad. I needed him to affirm how much strength it took to be honest about something so difficult. I needed confirmation of the wisdom of my choice to be open about who I was. And I needed to explore myself and my sexuality without anyone telling me that straight was the better way to go. (These guidelines and others are spelled out in my book *Gay Affirmative Therapy for the Straight Clinician*.[1])

Not Lethal or Contagious

There are three typical patterns LGBTQ individuals follow in order to avoid their families' rejection or abandonment.[2] One is to maintain rigid emotional—and often geographical—distance from the family. LGBTQ children may run away from home for a life on the streets—particularly in their teen years, when they're young enough to get involved in hustling. They may simply move to another state, keeping their gayness away from the family and visiting very rarely.

The second is "Don't ask, don't tell." The LGBTQ child stays connected to his or her family, but "the elephant in the room" is never talked about by anyone. Everyone knows that "the friend" is more than a friend, but no one dares say so.

The third strategy is "It's okay to tell me but don't tell your father." The gay son is officially out to one parent or sibling, who responds with support but with a warning not to tell certain other family members.

Let me be definite and clear about a common misconception. *Family issues don't make a person gay.* As a psychotherapist, I've had the luxury of meeting many different kinds of men and women. I've treated many heterosexual men with the same background and childhood as mine, yet they have nary a gay bone in their bodies. How you were raised has little or nothing to do with your sexual and romantic orientation.

My parents needed to know that their son took such a big risk to tell them he was gay because he deeply valued the parent-child relationship. My parents needed to know *they* did not make me gay, that the news that I was gay couldn't "kill" anyone, and that it wasn't contagious. (I recall relatives actually warning me that if I told certain people, it might kill them or "They may decide to be gay themselves.")

Families need accurate information about homosexuality, not ignorance and misinformation. My family needed to know about those adolescent suicides linked to sexuality issues. They needed to hear that it was perfectly okay for them to disagree with me about my gayness—and to talk to me about it openly.

It's acceptable to have differences within a family, but when there's no communication, problems always arise.

Nick, age 27, was a well-adjusted young man with a promising future as a layout artist. Some years before, he had told his family—Southern Methodists who attended church regularly—that he was gay.

Nick's father wasn't at all accepting: "I didn't raise you to be a faggot. If you live in sin, I want nothing to do with you." (I've actually had parents tell me that they would have preferred that their child be a murderer than gay.)

For many years since his father told him this, Nick had kept quiet about his gayness. Now, however, he had grown tired of the silence. He entered into therapy with me to deal with his overwhelming feelings of sadness and grief over his father's rejection.

He decided he needed to talk, even it if meant being disowned for good. He'd come to realize that his silence was causing him much distress and that he needed to put the issue to rest by making a move himself.

And talk he did. He made several attempts to speak to his father, but his father would have none of it. Finally he looked Nick in the eye and said, "I no longer have a son," and slammed the front door in Nick's face.

Nick was devastated. During an emergency phone call with me soon after, he sobbed as he told me what had happened. Not long afterward, he went to court and legally changed his last name to cut all ties to his father and his family.

Today, Nick has found peace within himself. He has no regrets and, more than anything, he feels sorrow for his father.

How the Family Handles Secrets

In most families, the existing dynamics become exaggerated when a son comes out. Telling your family you are gay plunges them into a temporary crisis. When in crisis, people revert to old, familiar behaviors—dysfunctional or not.

If the family is religious, for example, they might become more devout. If there's alcoholism, there might be even more drinking. If family relations were strained before, they become even more distant. Family members tend to blame it all on their gay son. Worse, the gay man tends to believe he is somehow responsible for his family's adverse reaction and dysfunction.

There's a favorite aphorism among therapists who treat gay clients: "When a child comes out of the closet, the family goes in." For the family to acknowledge "Our child is gay" can be just as high an emotional hurdle as the one the child faced before coming out to them. Just as LGBTQ individuals pass through stages of coming out, their families can go through similar stages.

Healthy families address difficult issues with open discussions and sensitivity. In that case, any controversial issue—such as telling them you're gay—will be easier to deal with. Many different truths can exist in these families without anyone feeling threatened.

A kind of group energy forms in families, too. Each family member is affected by your coming out, but also by other members' reactions. Family members may do anything to get you to *change back* to who you used to be so they don't have to face the truth about you or about themselves.

This "change-back" syndrome becomes most obvious among the old drinking buddies of a recovering alcoholic. When the group socializes, friends might offer the man in recovery something to drink, telling him, "One won't hurt, and you're probably not an alcoholic anyway." Admitting that a friend is in recovery can mean having to face one's own drinking problem.

When the truth is spoken, other uncomfortable and unexamined truths tend to "come out of the closet"—which makes the core issue seem even heavier than it already is. I've had clients talk about how, after they told their families they were gay, other family secrets spilled out.

The Child Is Not to Blame

Frank was a 33-year-old man referred to me following a "nervous breakdown." He had become overly anxious at his job as manager of a large hotel—which was anxiety-provoking in and of itself. As a result, he was psychiatrically hospitalized for depression and anxiety.

Never married, Frank identified himself as homosexual. He stated that during his therapy in the hospital, his therapist asked why he identified himself as homosexual and not gay. Frank didn't have a good answer for that. He was out to himself but not to anyone else locally. For a while he had lived in New York City, where he was out as a gay man to all of his friends. He admitted that he was more comfortable being gay, but his job in Manhattan didn't work out, so he returned home and went back into the closet.

Frank reported coming from a loving but not demonstrative family. He'd had a turbulent relationship with his father, who died when Frank was still in his teens. Because love wasn't openly expressed, Frank thought the neglect was his fault. He had long known he was "different," and he feared that if his parents learned about this "part of him," they might reject him. So he kept to himself, pulling away from both parents. He and his father were arguing at the time of his death and never resolved the conflict. That was also Frank's "fault."

I'm always deeply concerned when clients try to take the blame for their childhood problems. It is overwhelming for a child to believe that his parents—the adults—are not handling things, so he unconsciously makes himself the culprit.

During our work together, I coached Frank to consider coming out, starting with his family. We talked about how his "nervous breakdown" was a result of keeping his romantic and sexual orientation a secret. Frank began to develop a more affirmative self-concept and to identify himself as gay, not homosexual.

Ultimately, he decided to tell his mother. They cried together. A very religious woman, she urged him to try various programs in their church that offered hope and promised change. Frank told her he didn't want to change and that he was happy being gay. Then she disclosed information that was news to Frank. She said Frank's father had been a very jealous, domineering man and had competed for her attention after their five children were born. The youngest, a boy, was born with Down Syndrome. Jealous of the amount of time his wife devoted to the child, the father demanded the child be put up for adoption. The mother agreed.

Frank also learned that when he was an infant, his father insisted that Frank be placed with his maternal aunt so that he and

Frank's mother could both go to work. Until he was three years old, Frank lived with his aunt during the week and came home periodically.

This was very significant. Children form deep bonds with their primary caregivers in the first eighteen months. Not surprisingly, Frank always felt closer to his aunt than to his own mother. Why his mother didn't take Frank home at night during the week or on weekends isn't clear, but Frank believed his pathologically jealous father was most likely glad to have his "competition" out of his home. Frank wasn't rejected by his father for being gay. His father was already full of rejection.

Coming out to his mother not only freed Frank to be more open as a gay man, but also let him understand his family dynamics more fully. I assure my clients that their being gay isn't anyone's fault or responsibility. Gayness is not the result of anything anyone did or said. It is something you learn to be comfortable with, and your decision to come out lets you live your life with fewer emotional hindrances.

Be Ready Before You Come Out

It's imperative that you feel good about being gay at the time you tell your family. I've found that if clients come out before they are ready, their families pick up on their ambivalence and raise doubts and difficult questions. If you're not fully self-actuated as a gay man, and your family engages in "change-back" behavior, you might spend even more time struggling.

I was 18 years old when I came out to my family, and I was very angry. My therapist, who was helpful in other ways, led me to believe my gayness was a consequence of having a smothering mother and a distant father. If my parents had been different, he reasoned, I would have been straight. So when I came out to my parents, I blamed them for my situation. I blamed my mother for being overprotective, and told my father it was his fault I was gay because he'd left us to start a new family when I was three.

I was angry and wanted them to feel bad. We all went screaming into family therapy—this time with a new therapist who also believed that being gay was the result of shoddy parenting. She asked, "Joe, why would you tell your family? And number two, why did you tell them in this way?"

I was horrified and didn't answer her because I felt shamed. She and my other therapists insisted I should change, but of course I couldn't, no matter how hard I tried. What I really needed to hear was how brave and courageous I was for telling.

The result of all this was that I went back in the closet, got a girlfriend, and lived an outward life as a heterosexual, while I secretly pursued an underground gay life. Ultimately, at age 21, I found the courage to finally open that closet door, let my parents off the hook, and be responsible for my own life by presenting my gayness in a healthy way. My family was more accepting the second time around. I believe we spent more time healing from what therapy did to us than from my coming out.

When Will was 14 years old, he got on the Internet and started chatting with gay men. Inevitably, the talk became sexual. One day, Will's parents looked at the history of his Web activity and discovered that he had been looking at gay porn sites. They also learned he was exchanging emails with gay men, some of whom were very sexually forward.

They were shocked. The family went to a therapist, who told them that Will didn't have an issue with his *gayness* but rather with his *parents*, who needed to come to terms with the fact that their son was gay. How could a 14-year-old know his sexual and romantic orientation, they wondered. The therapist helped them see that straight, gay, and bisexual teenagers come to know their orientation in similar ways.

Will's parents went to PFLAG (Parents, Friends and Family of Lesbians and Gays), which has numerous chapters across the country. Most of the members are straight, but many gays and lesbians attend. Within a matter of weeks, they recognized that Will was gay and accepted his gayness lovingly. They took Will to gay groups, supported his being authentically himself, and became increasingly involved in PFLAG.

Will ultimately developed healthy self-esteem as a gay teen. He went to college and is now a happy gay man. His parents offered him true support and didn't let their own agenda override their son's. In so doing, they gave Will a much better chance of adjusting to his gay sexual and romantic orientation than if they had decided to fight him or place their desires ahead of his.

Being Gay Shouldn't Be a Secret

There's a difference between privacy and secrecy. Some things are none of our parents' business and should be kept private, but being gay isn't one of them. Not telling them you are gay is secrecy, and as Alcoholics Anonymous says, "Secrets keep us sick."

Secrets also keep us feeling ashamed. To be a fully out and confident gay man means telling your parents—though not if they might injure or abuse you in some way. When violence or other life-threatening issues are at stake, then your motive becomes self-protection. In such a case, it makes sense not to tell. Also, if you're dependent on them and you think they'll abandon you, then it also might make sense not to tell. Otherwise, let the differences in your family exist—risk their adverse responses. Speak *your* truth to your parents, whatever that truth is.

As with any family disagreement, often you'll need a "time out." If your family needs to distance themselves from you, give them their space. This is an act of love and courage on your part.

"Why did you tell us?" they might ask. "Are you trying to hurt us? Why did we need to know this?" Some of my clients' parents tell them, "It's just a phase," or "If you chose that lifestyle, I just don't want to hear about it." Sometimes, they just ignore the issue. "What else is new in your life?"

Many clients say that their being gay doesn't affect their parents, so they don't need to know. I disagree. Bringing over a boyfriend or a partner as "just a friend"—or not bringing him at all—means keeping secrets. That jeopardizes your relationship with everyone involved.

Usually not disclosing who you are is a result of your own reluctance to confront your family. Be truthful and say, "I choose not to tell my parents because I don't wish to face their reaction." You'll grow more as a person from that place of honesty than if you claim, "They don't need to know," simply to dodge the issue.

Of course, my family would have been relieved had I stayed quiet about this part of my life for good. In the movie *Torch Song Trilogy*, Arnold (Harvey Fierstein's character) fights with his mother, played by Anne Bancroft. She accuses him of pushing his sex life down her throat. He turns to her and says, "If you want to be in my life, I am not editing out the things you don't like." That line is very important. I show this film clip when I give talks and wherever families come to try to understand their children's gayness.

Fusion and Differentiation

The therapist Murray Bowen was a pioneer in family therapy. He developed the model now known as *Bowen Theory* to help individuals achieve and maintain their own identity in interpersonal family relationships.

Bowen noticed in his therapy sessions that families with problems tended to be unusually reactive to one other. They seemed to be overly influenced by one another's thoughts and feelings, and had usually adopted ways to avoid each other. (As we've seen, gay men often distance themselves from their families as a way to avoid coming out to them.) Bowen's idea was that this hyper-reactivity arises from a failure to gain mature independence from others' feelings and thoughts.

Bowen developed two concepts: *fusion*—unhealthy togetherness without boundaries—and *differentiation*, the ability to take an "I" position in one's family of origin. The "I" position enables one to define one's own position in an autonomous but nonreactive way. A critical point in Bowen's theory is that differentiation isn't achieved through breaking off relationships out of reactivity. "Cut-offs" sometimes imply reactivity, just like fusion.[1]

Bowen concluded that family members have a right to say "yes" to what feels appropriate for them and "no" to what doesn't. He didn't believe in relationships with no boundaries.

I agree with Bowen's conclusions about the importance of families staying in dialogue with one another, even when they disagree. My experience as a therapist convinces me that being open and honest with your family is a move toward stronger ties, as is allowing them their own reactions.

The only reaction that's *not* acceptable is blame. All members must be able to express their opinions honestly—but without the intent to wound. If wounding or blaming occurs, then self-preservation, not reactivity, prompts a cut-off. And that is appropriate.

In the extreme case that family members are prone to physical violence or addictive behaviors, and won't remedy the problem or get help, then you are justified in protecting yourself. When you try to work out difficult issues with your family, do they continue to disrespect you? Are they unwilling to change their behavior or take responsibility for their part in a dysfunctional relationship? Do you keep going back, only to get emotional and mental abuse each time? Cut-offs under these circumstances are not reactive or immature. Keeping your distance to protect yourself makes sense.

If family members say they want to mend and heal, but don't want to be accountable for their role in the problem, this will make any relationship with them unsafe. They will say things like, "I am not doing it intentionally" or "You are being too sensitive" or deny their role completely and say, "I don't know what the problem is" even though you have told them repeatedly. Focusing on your family's behaviors more than on what they say can often indicate the truth about how they feel about you. It may just mean they cannot say it or admit it to themselves and consequently to you.

You may have to remove yourself from a destructive family environment to find a more secure way to deal with it. Sometimes, resolving family differences means extremely limited contact. Making this decision in non-reactive ways is nothing more than self-preservation.

Using Bowen's model, a gay man who comes out to his family is growing, separating in a healthy way, and letting his loved ones have their emotions even as he retains his own sense of self. In doing so, he not only helps himself and his family enjoy healthier relations, but he also better prepares himself for the differences he will encounter in a relationship with a partner.

Bowen defined self-differentiation as the state when family members are together, yet separate. Self-differentiation lets parents and children maintain their own identities apart from the family as a whole. Balancing love with the need for personal space creates self-differentiation. This is what it means to set healthy limits.

If love and limits aren't balanced, then the forces of separateness and togetherness become unstable. Family members can become self-centered, cruel to one another, overly rebellious, and disrespectful. They lack interest in one another, are emotionally cut off from the family, express false emotions and thoughts, have difficulty trusting, feel rejected, and suffer low self-esteem. If togetherness outweighs the force of separateness, members can become jealous, emotionally over-involved, punish all negative feelings, and feel rejected for being different.

Some therapists put too much emphasis on the need for separateness. One talk-show host (who should know better) advises her callers to break contact with people who don't "behave" without trying to work things out first. In a healthy family, togetherness should be in balance with separateness. In an unhealthy family, one force outweighs the other.

Meredith, a 42-year-old mother, came to see me when her 20-year-old son, Roger, told her he was gay. She was sure this wasn't so. Her husband, Roger's stepfather, wasn't interested in attending therapy, so she came to the appointment with Roger.

Meredith started out by stating that Roger "didn't know what he was" and struggled with his sexual identity. She wanted to provide some help. Roger had come out to her only two months before, and Meredith was still devastated. She confessed that Roger, her youngest, was closer to her than were her other two children. She even stated that she felt closer to Roger than to her own husband.

Roger assured her that nothing had changed and that he loved just her as much as before. He said that he was *not* in fact struggling with his sexual identity. He knew for sure that he was gay.

Meredith took this as an affront. "Why are you trying to hurt me like this?" she asked. Over the course of several sessions, it became clear that Meredith's relationship with her second husband had been weak for years. She had given very little to the marriage and received little in return. She had devoted all of her energy to her daughter and two sons.

Roger's brother and sister had moved to other parts of the country, which she took as personal rejections: "I never believed I couldn't see my kids every day." Yet they remained in constant contact with her and visited her four times a year. That was not enough for her. She felt alone and abandoned. Now, Roger had told her he was gay and he was spending less time with her. Understandably.

Although PFLAG offers parents of gay children the opportunity to connect with each other, she would not attend PFLAG meetings unless Roger went with her, and she refused to talk with any other parent when she was at a meeting. (Her husband refused to have anything to do with PFLAG.)

As a therapist, I saw problems everywhere. This family placed a tremendous overemphasis on togetherness. Meredith had centered her life on her children, who were now adults trying to achieve separateness.

I assured her that her children's departure from the nest and regular contact were signs of her good parenting. Her children felt secure enough to make lives for themselves. But Meredith insisted these were *not* positive signs. I also praised her for having raised a gay son who was willing to share his authentic self with her. This didn't calm her either, so we moved on to the real, underlying issues.

Her recent life had centered on her daughter and sons because of her "distant" marriage. Now that the nest was empty, her chilly marriage left her feeling lonely and angry.

I asked Howard, Meredith's husband, to come to our next appointment. He did —reluctantly. Though he wouldn't participate in our conversations, I gave him credit for showing up.

Roger was comfortably gay. His main issue was his mother, who was troubled over "losing" her son and suffering in a marriage that needed work. I told them Roger was on his way to a healthy gay identity, and the issue was really about their need to come to terms with having a gay son and living in a marriage based on parallel lives. Howard worked long hours and was an avid fisherman. Meredith had repeatedly asked him to spend more time with her, but Howard had resisted. I concluded that if therapy were to continue, it should focus on Howard and Meredith, which sent a message to the whole family.

Roger had done a good thing by coming out to his family, speaking the truth, and prompting Howard and Meredith to examine their own relationship.

As she became more confident about herself, Meredith was no longer so emotionally needy with her children. She also developed healthier connections with other friends and relatives. She and Howard eventually resolved the issues in their marriage—all thanks to Roger's integrity and courage. Coming out is a good thing for the whole family.

References

1. Joe Kort. *Gay Affirmative Therapy for the Straight Clinician: The Essential Guide*. New York: W. W. Norton & Company, 2008.
2. Michael E. Kerr and Murray Bowen. *Family Evaluation: An Approach Based on Bowen Theory*. Toronto: Penguin Books, Canada, 1988.

Chapter 4

Graduate from Eternal Adolescence

Would the small boy you once were look up to the man you have become?

—Author unknown

Some psychotherapists and mental health professionals used to assume that being gay or lesbian is just a form of delayed adolescence. They believed that gays haven't "evolved" to the "natural" state of heterosexuality, and because we gay people are emotionally and psychologically stuck in our teens, we can't mature into wholly functional adults.

There's absolutely no truth to this. But unfortunately, gay culture does sometimes discourage growing up.

Between the ages of 12 and 18, teenagers must grapple with issues of intimacy and sexuality. During their psychological development, they normally date many peers, experiment with sex and mind-altering substances, and generally act up. Their friends become their new family. They begin to assert themselves, often in a moody, anti-adult way. The gay man who's coming out also goes through a period of rebellion—except that the experience has been postponed until his adult years.

Just as a teenager *should* develop his own identity—which sometimes means rebelling against his family's values—the newly out gay man no longer abides by the dominant culture's expectations of him. Indeed, a gay man *has* to be rebellious to carve out a place for himself in a heterocentric world. He follows his own line of reasoning, which is not necessarily compatible with what makes sense to others. For any adolescent, emotional and sexual intimacy is the primary goal—just as for the gay man in Stage Five of coming out.

Unfortunately, society looks at this delayed developmental stage in gay men and, through the lens of heterosexism, sees only an adult carrying on like a teenager—being radical, sexually promiscuous, angry, and immature. The result is a sweeping generalization: "That's just how gay men are." Because these behaviors are so visible, homophobic and homonegative writers and mental health experts have decided that this is the "gay lifestyle." They label all gay men as immature and developmentally stunted and refuse to follow the transitional stage to the end of its cycle.

But like most straight men who reach their middle 20s, gay men eventually settle down, feel more comfortable with themselves, and become less "in your face." In Stage Six of the coming-out process, a gay man integrates his beliefs and his identity with the rest of society and no longer calls so much attention to himself. He is emotionally grown-up.

Most adults—particularly parents who've been unsuccessful in developing their own sexual intimacy—are uncomfortable with adolescents' apparent success in this regard. With some jealousy, they view teenagers' demonstrative, assertive sexuality as adversarial and disobedient. But through their disrespectful behavior, teens are striving to separate themselves from their families and to become individuals with their own values and beliefs. This can be frightening to parents who don't know where their journey will lead.

This is also the case for gays and lesbians in Stage Five. They begin to separate and individuate, and suddenly they find themselves struggling against negative energy from the heterocentric culture, just like a teenager who starts to resist the constraints his family places on him. As a young boy, I enjoyed being Jewish. But at age 8, if I didn't enjoy it, I could never have told my mother, "Look, I'm not keen on Hebrew school, so I want to go to catechism and be baptized a Catholic." She would never have allowed it—and very few Jewish families would.

Until puberty, our caretakers make us comply with their expectations of us. Then, as teens, our task is to find out who we really are. This is why coming out is so important. You can now appreciate that any man who's still in the closet is living according to Mommy and Daddy's expectations. He hasn't become his own man. But even after coming out, he often leaves other problems in the closet behind him—although they never stay there!

Women Can Be Role Models for Maturity

For gay men who fail to complete the adolescent stage, too many problems arise for me to cover in one chapter. There's OCSB (next chapter), which begins as any adolescent's "normal" experimental stage but can develop into persistent problematic sexual behaviors. But let me note for emphasis: Having problems with excessive sexual behaviors isn't a gay issue; it's a *guy* issue.

Even so, straight men generally have mothers, girlfriends and wives who help them to grow from boys into heterosexual adults. We gay men usually lack mentors and role models (see Chapter 6). Most of us experience no social pressure to force the issue and to compel us to "grow up."

Time and again in my practice, I see wives who want their men to be more involved as fathers and husbands. Traditional male culture emphasizes competition, hunting, and scoring with women—all solitary pursuits. It's no surprise that so many men— gay, bisexual, and straight—do a fine job in their careers but not in their adult relationships.

I've found that lesbians are more grown-up than most gay males. Both in and out of my practice, I see more empathy, attentiveness, connectedness, and maturity within their relationships. We men have a lot to learn!

In general, girls mature faster than boys. We see this even during early development: Little girls talk earlier, are romantically interested earlier than boys—and are typically attracted to older partners. It's common for a heterosexual girl to have a crush on a boy who's still hanging out with his male buddies and doesn't even know that girls exist. Not until later do boys catch up to girls' emotional maturity. Thus it makes sense that lesbians are more mature than gay men. Lesbians tend to be more serious about their lives and more organized and political. Unfortunately, many lesbians go the extreme and find it difficult to have fun or relax.

Lesbian comedian Shan Carr recounts working on an all-gay cruise ship, where two militant lesbians found themselves at the ship's bar with the comedian and a gay male friend of hers. He was eating Cheddar Goldfish from a bowl, and she was munching on peanuts. He turned to Shan and said, "Isn't this funny—you're eating nuts, and I'm eating fish!"

Both laughed. The two militant lesbians screamed, "*WE DO NOT TASTE LIKE FISH!*"

When Shan Carr told this joke, her audience roared.

"Some lesbians," said Carr, "don't know how to let go and have some fun with gay-and-lesbian differences." True, but lesbians do know how to get down to serious business in their lives and relationships.

My husband and I have been on several gay cruises. The ships' crews have usually been predominately heterosexual. One captain told us at the "meet the captain" reception that he and the crew look forward to these cruises, because we gay men "have fun, spend a lot of money, and don't complain." Crewmembers have told me they have a great time with us gay men and look forward to attending our parties.

I agree: Gay men do have a lot of fun, but often it's unbalanced—too much fun and not enough seriousness. I do think there's a time and place for fun and sex, but endless adolescence gets in our way. Truth is, many of us gay men abandon relationships once the painful work begins. Unlike lesbians, who generally manage to channel their anger into political activity, we gay men tend to repress our anger and difficult feelings for other men. Pleasurable feelings are allowed to surface and become sexualized. Instead of dealing with our anger directly, we tend to express it through easy sexual hookups.

As Mean As High School

Our anger also may come out sideways when we're rude and critical of other gay men. In my work with gay men and in the gay community, I find that while we might not complain to heterosexual staff or business owners, we complain a lot about one another. In fact, we have a tendency to be quite mean—just as in high school. On one gay cruise, I heard men bash the cruise's gay sponsors, who were "in it for the money" and "not genuine." In the same breath the men expressed humble gratitude for the heterosexual crew's having us on "their" boat.

Are we afraid to see our peers reaching success before us? Isn't there room for all of us? As we mature, we see that any man who makes a good living by doing something for our community is just as respectable as the heterosexual who does the same thing.

I believe that, unconsciously, we gay men allow heterosexuals their traditional privileges and attack ourselves for wanting the same. This comes from our not getting respect and support early in our lives. We have to claim the respect we deserve and resist the impulse to attack other gay men.

We are a *community* of men who've been physically bashed and emotionally abused for being gay. Unfortunately, just as we begin to recover from the effects of that abuse, we begin to take it out on one another. Just like teenagers, we form our own peer groups and cliques. Those who are good-looking and in shape become popular; those who aren't attractive are marginalized. At a party, I heard another gay man making fun of an overweight guy: "He's so big he needs his own zip code." I know the target of his remark overheard him—and I'm sure the jokester meant to be heard.

Teenagers often judge each other harshly, to cover up their own pain. As they struggle to free themselves from parental domination, they join peer groups and decide who is in or out. Gay men do the same, and they can be just as mean-spirited.

Many minorities have the same tendency to attack one another. This is called *lateral discrimination*: The minority group internalizes the presumed superiority of the larger society, and individuals in the group act out toward one another.

If a gay man is out to only his gay friends, but not to the others in his life, he may not feel challenged to move ahead. Similarly, if teenagers are isolated in their peer groups and don't have adults to help them, they won't pass through the rebellious stage in healthy ways. As gay men, we lack healthy role models to challenge us to develop concern for others—a part of the growing-up process that typically occurs during adolescence. But heterosexism and homophobia teach us not to have concerns for other gays and lesbians—only for heterosexuals.

Gay teenagers learn to avoid each other and to envy their heterosexual peers, because heteronormative values are instilled in most children and teenagers. Consequently, gays and lesbians receive no information about how to deal with one another romantically and socially. We're left to cultivate humane regard for one another on our own.

If he's lucky, the man (or teenager) stuck in adolescence will hear, "You'll thank me for this someday," from parents, grandparents, and others who step in to identify his adolescent behavior and challenge him to move on into adulthood. Sadly, few gay men have people to push them toward maturity. Heterosexuals who don't have an older brother or sister can watch a child star like Ron Howard or Jodie Foster successfully progress to adulthood. We seldom have the opportunity to watch a gay boy turn into a gay teen and, finally, into a healthy gay adult.

The Party Needs to End
Gay men trapped in endless adolescence have a few common traits: They believe that when hard times come, someone will

rescue them. They long to be cared for as they were as children. And like children, they don't want to let the carefree times go.

We need to move on with our lives and assume adult responsibilities. This is no easy task, but one that everyone, gay or straight, has to face someday. Taking the easy way out only creates more trouble later on in life—for ourselves and for others.

For their social outlets, my "adolescent" clients go exclusively to bars where most of the men are very young and want even younger men. They spend money on things they don't need. They fly to outposts like Fire Island, Provincetown, or Key West. They squander time and frequent-flyer miles chasing big, lavish, weekend circuit parties where sex and drugs are prevalent.

When they attempt (if at all) to get together privately with their "bar friends," there's no connection. They prefer superficial, short-lived, long-distance relationships. As soon as things get rocky, they move onto someone else in another state, even another country. These men dress young and judge each other on their pecs, their abs, and whatever the parking valet just put in the garage. To keep their mind off the grim reaper, they use drugs and alcohol into their 30s, 40s, and 50s.

I don't justify substance abuse at any age, but a guy in his 20s can more easily recover from its effects. Otherwise, there's nothing wrong about circuit parties or enjoying the company of younger men, but sooner or later, the party's over. This necessary return to grown-up reality is frequently depicted in myths and fairy tales: At midnight, the coach turns back into a pumpkin that's too small for Cinderella to ride in. Only the glass slipper—her chance for a committed partnership—still "fits" her. Alas, too many gay men are still riding in pumpkins—they're unwilling to let go of what was important to them once, back in the days when they first came out. They hold their parents and society—but not themselves—responsible for correcting abuses and righting wrongs.

Growing Up Is Hard to Do

Growing up demands a realistic look at the world around us. It requires that we understand and accept that things are not fair. We need to re-examine the way we were raised and how our families function now, for good or for ill.

The tasks required for growing up are not easy. All too often, taking this closer look illuminates patterns of family dysfunction that are painful to acknowledge. To avoid this pain, we hang on to our illusions. It's easier to play the victim and complain that you have no control over a world that's out to get you. It's easier to keep looking for the unconditional love you didn't get from your family and stay out of long-term relationships that demand a growing, evolving maturity. However, by choosing the easy path, you miss out on so much of the richness and beauty life has to offer.

Eddie was a successful 42-year-old attorney who made very good money. Now that his parents were divorced, and his father no longer needed the big co-op apartment where he'd grown up, Eddie resented his father for not giving him the place. After all, hadn't his father's alcoholism ruined Eddie's childhood? And caused Eddie to delay his coming out? And make it difficult for him to stay in relationships?

With a strong sense of self-righteousness, Eddie didn't want to admit, much less examine, his own obvious capabilities as an adult. He certainly had every right to be disappointed. But his father had every right to do with the co-op whatever he liked.

Another client, Louis, often cheated on his partner. He didn't appreciate my feedback: I told him his secrecy about his flings— which made a lie of his agreement with his partner to be monogamous—showed a lack of integrity.

This lack of communication was part of a larger problem: Louis and his partner were having relationship problems, but they wouldn't talk them out. As a result, they fought constantly and had more than a few sexual difficulties. They began to harbor negative feelings toward one another, and their sex life suffered even more. Louis insisted he had the right to "go find other men who can meet my sexual needs, if he can't." If he discussed his problems openly and directly, his partner might tell him to leave. To avoid the risks and pains of conflict, Louis lived a double life and refused to be accountable to himself or his relationship.

What did these two clients have in common? As children, neither had his needs met. As a result, both continued to try to get adults to meet those needs—but in negative, acting-out ways. Some clients like Eddie keep going back to a parent who's unable or unwilling to give love and acceptance. When their efforts are thwarted (as they inevitably are), they usually turn to another authority figure—a boss, partner, sibling, or friend—and project their childhood problems onto this person. Of course, they expect this "surrogate" parent to supply whatever their real parents didn't give them. But the problem can never be fixed this way.

Your Childhood Is Over

The child you once were can't get his needs met in the present. Childhood's over—it's a done deal. Trying to get someone in the present to fulfill needs unmet in the past is not just inappropriate, but also impossible—a sure recipe for frustration and disappointment.

One time, while I was visiting my sister, I found it very difficult to understand what my two-year-old nephew was trying to say. "He wants a drink of water," my sister explained. I had no idea how she'd understood what he wanted, but she was just paying close attention, the way a mother should. Only in your early childhood can you expect others to listen to you that closely and to anticipate your needs and fight your battles for you. Now that you're an adult, it's not appropriate or realistic to expect anybody else to know what you want—you must speak up and ask for it. But even if you've built a good argument that makes sense, you might not get what you're asking for. Children are allowed temper tantrums; adults are not.

In his efforts to meet one of his childhood needs, Eddie kept bumping against the same wall: His father was still not interested in pleasing him. The same was true for Louis, who would rather go behind his partner's back than face the consequences of his own actions and choices.

Neither of these men could grow past adolescence until each felt the necessary pain of recognizing that his childhood needs weren't met and never would be. As an adult, each man needed to accept responsibility for taking care of himself. The other adults in their lives had plenty to handle on their own.

David, a divorced 43-year-old gay man with a grown daughter, sought treatment to help cope with his depression. He was now in Stage Six of coming out, where he had integrated with the mainstream culture. Several years before, he had gone through a very difficult divorce. Brenda, his ex-wife, had presented him as a villain for leaving her after a 20-year marriage. In an effort to compensate for what he saw as his wrongdoing—heterosexually marrying and then coming out of the closet—he offered her more money than even the court felt was appropriate. Although he made a decent amount of money from his dental practice, he found himself without enough money to meet his own needs.

When we explored his background, it came out that his narcissistic mother had run the family. She had taught her son that to get her love, he needed to please her and be her caretaker. David's father, largely uninvolved, acquiesced to whatever she demanded.

David never managed to please her. He wanted to become an architect, but she told him he'd never make good money and that he should become a dentist instead. David didn't like dentistry school. But when he went to his father for direction about changing career goals, his father said, "I won't pay for your education unless you become a dentist."

At the age of 22, David felt he had no other choice but to comply with other people's expectations. When he became an adult, this script stayed with him. He married Brenda, knowing he was gay. After 10 years of unhappy marriage he began to contemplate divorce, only to hear negative judgments from both his mother and wife: "How would it look for a man with a little child to divorce?" He stayed married to a wife who berated him constantly, called him names, told him he wasn't a good father, accused him of hiding money, and constantly demanded to know his whereabouts.

David felt his gayness acutely. He buried it under alcohol abuse, and took appointments on weekends to avoid going home. But he eventually received a wake-up call: Prostate cancer forced David to assess his life. He decided to stop using alcohol, and he entered a 12-step program for alcohol abusers. During his early recovery, he began to face some of the problems he'd avoided before. Now that his daughter was grown, he became increasingly intolerant of his wife's emotional abuse. His urge to come out of the closet grew stronger now that he no longer anesthetized his feelings with alcohol. Still, his situation caused him a great deal of anxiety. How could he let down his wife—and his parents, of course!—not only by coming out but also by reducing the family income? After their divorce, Brenda would have to take a job, and his daughter would have to fend for herself financially.

Through therapy, David discovered that his childhood family script still ruled his life. He'd never grown up—or more accurately, he had never outgrown the shame-induced docility that had been drummed into him as a boy. Looking back, he'd tried his best to follow the privileged heterosexual model to the letter: Get a lucrative education, get married, and make good money to support his family. The only problem was, he never wanted this scenario. He wanted to come out, find a satisfying relationship, and become an architect. But because of how those choices would have "looked," he elected to please everyone except himself. The tragedy, of course, was that he'd failed at that, too.

Now David was living on anti-depressant medication. His only way out was to challenge his family script and, while it wasn't an easy task, to learn that it was okay not to please others. He needed to confront his wife's, daughter's, and parents' judgments and not let them rule his life.

After many long months of therapy, David divorced Brenda. Even though he'd covered all his daughter's college expenses, she stopped talking to him because he stopped paying her car installments and credit card bills. He simply couldn't afford it. In addition, he had to admit that he'd given his child too much all along to compensate for the loving support he had never received from his own parents.

Next, David had to face an even harder challenge— confronting the family messages he'd received while growing up. His first response to my suggestion was, "I feel you're encouraging me to bash my parents." I wasn't, of course. Instead, I was inviting him to examine—for himself and on his own—his negative feelings about how he was raised. I wanted him to see how burying those feelings shaped his current life.

His mother and father, who strongly opposed his divorce, continued a relationship with Brenda. There was nothing wrong with their wish to see the mother of their granddaughter, but it *was* wrong of Brenda to continue to berate David and to put him down in front of their daughter.

Of course, David's parents telephoned him to describe the pain Brenda was going through. How could he inflict all this pain on her, they wondered, just to have sex with men? David needed to confront his parents. He initially told them, "Stop interfering in my life." Not listening, they replied, "This is our life, too, and Brenda is the mother of our grandchild."

Clearly, nothing David said or did would ever satisfy them. On top of everything else, they were angry because Brenda's mother snubbed them at church. In their view, this was all *David's* fault—fallout from his divorce. With my help, he decided to tell his parents that if they insisted on talking about Brenda or his former in-laws, he'd stop the conversation and hang up. They continued; he hung up. Over time, they learned not to bring these topics up with him. But for David, the process of learning to hold his ground was very difficult. He had to recognize that his parents weren't looking out for *his* best interests, but for their own. Their only concern was how his actions made them look in the eyes of their social associates. Now it was time for David to make *himself* feel good—and let his parents feel their own pain over his newfound independence.

Confronting Childhood Scripts

Remember, we all have two sets of parents: the ones who raised us and the internalized ones inside of us. We have to confront all the scripts we've followed since childhood. What fits now, and what doesn't? Abandoning scripts that no longer fit can be surprisingly painful. Are you disobeying and disrespecting what your parents want for you? Yes—moving away from adolescence requires that you disappoint others. Separation and individuation is what adulthood is all about. It's not disrespectful to honor your *own* journey. However, if your family threatens to reject you, it makes growth to adulthood vastly more challenging. This is just as true when you are coming out as when you're "out" on your own.

In graduating from endless adolescence, a son feels *separation guilt* over individuating from his family. Quite often, his family has given him subtle or overt messages that his separation will injure them. There are many jokes about the Jewish mother who states, "If you really loved me, you wouldn't leave me," but I don't think they're funny. I've seen the negative effects this kind of clinging has on clients trying to make an adult life for themselves.

Separation guilt is particularly common among clients who are *conflict avoidant*. Usually, they also have trouble living as openly gay men. And because they won't be more fully out, their partners often get frustrated or leave. They have few gay friends, because going to gay establishments causes them too much anxiety. They associate all these troubles with their belief that being gay is particularly difficult.

After some time in therapy, it becomes apparent that most of these men were raised in families where the message was, "Don't talk about your feelings, do as we say, and don't make waves." Being gay goes against a conflict-avoider's life script. Indeed, he'll do anything to avoid conflict—even if it means destroying his life. But a gay man *must* make waves in a society that wants gays to be quiet and that condemns people who live outside the norm.

Josh came to see me because he didn't feel much of anything about anything in his life. He had come out, but he'd never felt good about his homosexuality. He was in a relationship with a man, but he was ambiguous about it. He also wasn't attracted to women, romantically or sexually, which troubled him greatly.

He attributed this to homophobia and heterosexism, but there was more to his story. Josh's alcoholic father had abused his wife and kids verbally and physically. Many times, Josh listened to his father's rages after a night of drinking and came downstairs to find the living room turned upside down. One time, after his father beat her, his mother was taken to the hospital.

Josh's father saw anything that went against his demands as a threat. If Josh talked back, his father either intimidated him or beat him. Early on, Josh learned not to make waves that could precipitate violence. During his teenage years, he never rebelled. Nor did he establish a separate sense of self.

When Josh was 14, his father divorced his mother and married a woman with whom he'd been having an affair and who had children of her own. Josh's father considered them his new "family." Abandoned and rejected, Josh felt he hadn't been a good enough son and had caused his father to leave.

Children often make themselves "bad" to absolve their errant parents—they blame themselves for their feelings of rejection and pain. In his 20s, Josh knew better than to come out. He knew his father would be angry and might even incite the rest of the family to reject him, too. His mother hadn't protected him as a child— why would she defend him now?

Josh dated women and tried to make a go of heterosexuality. His attempts to be a "good boy" pleased his family, but not him. Then Josh joined a men's choir group, where he befriended some gay men. He liked them, became closer to them, and began to realize he was gay. But here, of course, he ran into trouble. Being gay meant going against the rules of a heterocentric society—and his family's rules as well. Now in his 30s, Josh had lived his entire life as an obedient son who always followed the rules and who became angry at people who didn't.

Then, at 36, he met Jack and started a relationship. But after several years together, Josh still didn't feel love for his partner or comfort with his gay identity. In therapy, he recognized that as a youngster he'd made an unconscious decision to behave like the "best little boy in the world" to avoid conflict, trouble, and beatings. Even if he hadn't been gay, Josh knew he would eventually have to risk his family's disapproval to be true to his values. His fundamentalist father and stepbrother often made disparaging comments about LGBTQ individuals. How could Josh admit he was one of those who were "all going to hell"?

His gay life was the main arena in which he acted out these conflicts. As his relationship with Jack progressed, the sexual side of their relationship dwindled until Josh was no longer interested in sex. This occurred about three months after they met. Typically, sexual feelings diminish within the first six to eighteen months after a relationship begins—Josh's rapid loss of interest was unusual. Throughout his life, Josh had viewed sex as bad and as dirty, in fact, he aspired to be asexual. Why?

Josh's story is typical of gay men who seek to avoid conflict. His father's violence and his mother's passivity had taught him that disapproval meant physical abuse and rejection.

He knew he should be angry with his father, but didn't feel it. Conjuring up any direct anger, he felt guilty, as if he were "bashing" the man. To protect his father, Josh had generalized his anger toward the world. In our therapy appointments, Josh often raged against the government, whose laws didn't offer protection to LGBTQ citizens, and he talked about feeling "powerless" and "helpless." This type of anger is necessary and appropriate, but Josh's overreaction ate at him and left him anxious and depressed. He languished in an unsatisfying, low-paying job, lived a secret, closeted life, and lacked emotion and sexual passion.

For Josh, having sex with another man meant having to admit he was gay. By shutting down his sexuality on the grounds that sex was "nasty and dirty," Josh kept himself developmentally at age 14, when his father divorced his mother to marry another woman. He was psychologically stuck in that time of his life.

He couldn't feel love for his partner, because he hadn't gone through the intimacy stage of development—the normal, healthy time when teenagers begin to form attachments to people outside their families. As a child, Josh had decided never to seek relationships outside his family. His dependence on them made it difficult for him to acknowledge what they'd done to him.

In individual therapy, Josh grew defensive about his family and was very protective of them. In group, he defended the parents of other group members, even as the members recounted the dysfunctional and abusive things their families had done to them. Whenever a group member had a breakthrough, Josh questioned the validity of therapy and discounted its effectiveness. "We're being brainwashed," he'd shout, even though he knew that wasn't true. He was a neutered, scared, depressed, and angry man who'd let his father and mother off the hook.

Josh said, "That's the past. It's over. Let's move on." I agreed, but I also argued that he couldn't move on until he learned to allow himself to enjoy adult sexuality, an intimate relationship with a partner, and the satisfaction that comes with resolving conflicts. This was the crux of his problem. By living as an asexual underachiever, Josh successfully kept himself "bad" in order to let his parents remain "good" in his mind.

Survivor guilt arises when you achieve more than your parents did. Originally, the term was used to describe the emotions felt by those who survived the Holocaust when other loved ones or family members did not. For related reasons, adult children can find it very difficult to leave home. They know they must go on with their lives, but leaving their parents behind is profoundly disturbing. I've had clients who sabotaged their own careers lest they become more successful than their parents—which was taboo, according to the message their parents had sent them. *Why should you have things any better than me?*

My client Max came from a lower middle-class background and rose to prominence in his marketing career. His partner was a worldly man who understood the finer things in life. One night, the two of them accompanied Max's parents to a restaurant that didn't serve alcohol, but encouraged patrons to bring their own. At the liquor store, Max's mother selected an inexpensive wine she enjoyed. Max and his partner—a wine connoisseur—selected one of the imported vintages they'd grown to like.

Max's mother saw the price and asked, "Why buy something so expensive, when the cheaper wine is just the same?"

Max explained why the expensive wine tasted better and that they'd learned to enjoy it.

"Well," she said, "don't forget the time when you were broke and didn't know anything. So don't think you can fool me with your wine connoisseur talk."

Max was crushed. How could his own mother say something so insulting? I explained that this had been her way of communicating that he hadn't grown bigger or better than the rest of his family. Threatened with his newfound knowledge, she engaged in "change-back" behavior (as discussed in Chapter 3)— she tried to change Max back into the man he was originally. Once he understood this, her remarks no longer bothered him.

Explaining this makes it all sound simple, but I know it's not. Gay and straight alike, all children are hardwired to be loyal—to protect their parents and not to hold them accountable. It can be extremely painful to reflect on the negative, abusive things your parents have done. It's not a question of bashing or blaming, but of identifying facts. It's not about making your parents right or wrong, good or bad—everyone's a little of both—but about looking at your real feelings about your childhood and moving forward into adulthood.

For gay men, the journey goes even farther. In his autobiography, *The Best Little Boy in the World*, Andrew Tobias writes about his efforts to conceal his gayness, about which he was most ashamed. In addition, the "best little boy" dared not speak a negative word about his parents, lest he be abandoned, rejected, or physically harmed.[1]

The way out of adolescence is to confront our childhood messages and challenge their validity in our lives today. Does that mean addressing the issues with your parents or childhood caretakers directly? Possibly. It definitely means confronting your internalized parents and caretakers—the ones who live inside of you, as you'll see in Chapter 7. But it can also be healing and helpful to sit down with your parents and "kick around" things you remember from childhood. It's important for your inner gay child to see that he's not little any longer, and that his parents aren't superhuman, but just people, like he is.

For most people this is dangerous territory. Like Josh, many clients believe I'm advising them to be hateful to their parents. I hear questions like, "My parents are old now. What's the point?" or "They're so good to me now. Why bring up all the hurtful things they did in the past?" In sessions with me, clients often find that simply talking about their parents—simply reviewing the facts and feeling the pain attached to those facts—makes them feel guilty. The facts make it impossible for them to deny their parents' negative behavior. Inevitably, negative feelings follow.

In addition, they get in touch with their grief—about what their parents did not do for them and were unable to give them in childhood. In her best-selling book, *The Drama of the Gifted Child*, Alice Miller addresses how children adapt to their parents' needs in order to please them, even at a very early age.[2] In doing so, children lose their true identity and authentic selves. They learn not to feel their most intense feelings, knowing these feelings are considered undesirable by their parents. Miller believes, as do I, that once this grief and pain is addressed in adulthood, a "new authority" over one's self emerges. Until people recognize and accept what they did and didn't get from their childhood, they cannot move forward in their therapy. Nor can they enter adulthood in a full, satisfying way.

References

1. Andrew Tobias (first published under the pseudonym John Reid), *The Best Little Boy in the World*, 25th Anniversary edition. New York: Ballantine Books, 1993.
2. Alice Miller. *The Drama of the Gifted Child: The Search for the True Self.* New York: Basic Books, 1981.

Chapter 5

Explore Erotic Turn-ons And Sexual Interests

If you go to war with your sexuality, you will lose, and end up in more trouble than before you started. I have never seen a single exception to this principle.

—Jack Morin, *The Erotic Mind*

Part 1: Healthy Gay Sex

Do You Have to Be So Anal?

Gay men may choose to express their sexuality in many different ways. The right way for you is the way that works best for you. Lots of gay men love anal sex. They identify as tops; they identify as bottoms; they identify as both. But you should understand that it is totally and perfectly fine if you never have anal sex.

Maybe you don't like it. It's not your thing. You're not a top; not a bottom. You're a "side." I wrote an article in *The Huffington Post* called "Guys on the 'Side': Looking Beyond Gay Tops and Bottoms."[1] Many gay men feel shame if they don't do anal sex. That's the result of ignorance and prejudice. No one should tell you what you ought to do.

This is also true for nonstandard sexual interests and behaviors that don't hurt anybody (yourself or others). Part of the luxury of being a gay man is permission to play with your fetishes openly, which is not the case for heterosexual men. For every twenty men with a fetish, there is only one woman. Heterosexual men have a lot more trouble finding play partners than we do.

Gay Sex vs. Guy Sex

It's true that some people say gay men are overly sexual, but I want to be clear: That's a *guy* thing, not a *gay* thing. If it were a gay thing, lesbians would be doing it, too. One benefit of being a gay man is that we get to have a lot of different kinds of sex that our heterosexual male counterparts don't. There's a freedom in that.

On the negative side, a culture without women does sometimes have problems with boundaries, with finding the "pause button." I had a male client once who answered a Craig's list ad: "My back door's open. Come fuck my mouth." Most women would never respond so casually to an invitation like that for quick anonymous sex. Women tend to want to know their partners. "Wait a minute. Let's learn each other's names. Let's go to dinner. Let's see if we like each other."

Many gay men are not into anonymous hookups or random sex, either. Often, these gay men feel ashamed about wanting a little courtship. I understand that they feel out of place, because it does appear that gay men are having sex everywhere, all the time. While that's the case for some gay men, it doesn't mean you have to do it. There's room for you, too. You're going to have to dig a little deeper and hunt a little more intentionally, but gay guys are out there who want what you want.

If you want to have sex in the context of a thoughtful, committed relationship, then that's what you should hold out for. When I was dating, I decided that having sex early with someone I was interested in was too painful if the relationship didn't work out. Being sexually intimate made me feel attached, and I was so disappointed if the other guy didn't feel the same. So, I started a "three-month rule." I wouldn't be sexual for the first three months of a relationship. We could kiss, dry hump, whatever … but with our clothes on. Some guys left me. If they couldn't explore our sexual compatibility right away, then they didn't want to stay, and I let them go. But my husband, Mike, was willing to give me that three-month window, and that's what drew me to him. I'm telling you my personal story, because I want you to really believe that it's okay for a single gay man to set sexual boundaries for himself.

What works for you is what's right for you. You might feel out of the norm, but being true to yourself is the only way to find what you truly want.

A lot of single gay men fear they'll never find someone who wants to be monogamous, because the gay community is so into open relationships. Therapist Michael Lasala[2] did research showing that 50 percent of gay male relationships are open. But 50 percent open means 50 percent closed. The feeling that you'll never find a monogamous gay partner is a heterosexist prejudice.

On the other hand, the belief that all relationships *should* be monogamous is also a heterosexist prejudice. If you're judgmental about it, which a lot of single gay men are, I ask you to look at your own internalized homophobia. What's wrong with people choosing to have open relationships? It may not be what *you* want, but if you condemn it for everyone, then that says more about you than the gay community. (I talk more about monogamy vs. non-monogamy in Chapter 6 of my book, *10 Smart Things Gay Men Can Do to Find Real Love*.[3] See also *Opening Up: A Guide to Creating and Sustaining Open Relationships* by Tristan Taormino.[4])

A Story About Open Gay Relationships

As you read the following story, check out how you feel. See if you have a strong reaction, a strong tendency to "take sides."

Alan and Brad were married and monogamous for seven years, and then they decided to open it up. They created a contract between themselves that specified the rules they would follow, including a rule about falling in love. If either detected anything

like love happening with anyone else, he was supposed to stop
playing with that person. In an open relationship, even though the
two parties are having sex with other people, it isn't "cheating" if
they're following their rules.

Soon, Alan and Brad were both spending a lot of time having
casual sex with random partners. After a few years, Alan became
very attached to one man, Carl, and Brad felt that Alan was in love
with him. Brad confronted Alan: "Our rule was to stop everything
once you started to fall in love." But Alan didn't think he was in
love. "It's just sex," he told Brad, "and I'm not going to stop
seeing Carl."

Their disagreement over Carl festered for a while, and then
they came to see me. Brad said, "I can't go on. I'm going to end
our relationship if Alan doesn't end this affair with Carl." Alan
protested. "I'm not having an affair. I'm not in love." Alan seemed
sincere, but soon it became obvious to me as a therapist that Brad
was right. Still, Alan wasn't convinced.

I worked with them for several months, and finally Alan told a
story in therapy that I thought I could use to help him see what was
going on. Alan had bought a gift for Carl, and he'd told Brad about
it. I said to Alan, "If you and Brad were a straight couple, and you
were the husband, and you were telling your wife that you bought
a gift for Carla and made a special trip to surprise her with it,
would you think that your wife would say, 'That's so cool. What
did you get for her? What was the look on her face when you gave
it to her? Was she surprised?' "

Alan said, "No, that would be preposterous."

"But that's the very thing you seemed to expect from Brad
when you told him about the gift you got for Carl."

And suddenly Alan saw the light. He understood, and he
agreed to end his relationship with Carl.

I always recommend a guideline for open relationships: Once
there's a breach of the contract, then close the relationship so that
you can repair it. Then, later, if you want to, you can reopen it, but
close it for a while just to bring back the connection. Also, I
recommend that if one person in the partnership feels there's been

a breach, then there's a breach. They need to push the pause button to talk about it.

The story of Alan and Brad continues. In therapy with me, they dealt with Brad's feelings of hurt and betrayal over the affair. After a year, they felt okay with each other again. Their trust was restored.

Besides the particulars of the affair, while their relationship was open, they had stopped having sex with each other. They were having sex only with other people. This is one of the dangers of having an open relationship, especially between gay men. If that's a decision you've made in your relationship, that's fine. It's not pathological in and of itself. It's pathological when one (or both) of the men in the couple misses having sex with the other.

Alan and Brad decided to open up the relationship again. They were coming to see me monthly, and everything was fine between them.

This story has a striking ending. One day, Alan came home and told Brad, "I had really hot sex with this guy, Dave." Alan showed Brad Dave's picture on Grindr, and Brad said "Oh my god, I was with that guy last month. And he *was* hot." Brad told Alan about his experience with Dave. Then, they both said almost at the same time to each other, "Wouldn't Dave be great for our friend Phil?" So they contacted Dave and set him up with Phil, who was single. And now they're all best friends, and they go on trips together.

I always say when I do training for straight therapists: "How many straight therapists in this room, and how many women, could imagine themselves in this story?" Everyone laughs, because they all know how rare it would be for a heterosexual story of open relationships to end up like this with two happy couples going on vacation together.

I like this story, because it illustrates the rich range of possibility in open relationships. An open relationship has benefits and difficulties not found in a closed relationship, and the difficulties don't mean the relationship is over or even the openness of the relationship is over.

I started this section with, "Check out how you feel as you're reading this story." Gay men with a lot of internalized homophobia tend to have a strong negative reaction: "See, this is what happens when you open a relationship. Gay men can't control themselves, and there is always trouble." And if that's what you found yourself thinking, I want you to catch yourself.

We gay men need to de-pathologize our sexuality. Check your homophobia. Be open to opportunities. It's okay if you don't care for open relationships. It's another thing if you have a strong negative visceral reaction: "This is wrong for everybody!" Ninety percent of that kind of visceral revulsion is about your negative conditioning, not about whether the challenges of open relationships are worthwhile or not.

To Grindr or Not to Grindr. That Is the Question.

Some gay men like to meet other men for quick hookups. There's nothing wrong with that. And on the other hand, if that's not your thing, it's okay not to want it. Grindr and other "gay apps" facilitate quick anonymous hookups, but these apps can also be used for dating and for finding friends.

You get to choose what works for you. For many gay men, especially when first coming out, the realization that there's so much easy access to hookups can cause a man to overdo it. And then he panics: "Every time I try to stop, I can't stop, or I stop and then I go back. OMG! I must be a sex addict." But most men would go a little crazy when first offered unlimited easy sex. Give a straight guy an opportunity to get on a heterosexual Grindr and see lots of women eager for hookups, and he would also experience a struggle. We know we're not wired for monogamy. Helen Fisher's work explains that.[5] (Also, see Chapter 6 of my *10 Smart Things Gay Men Can Do to Find Real Love.*) Struggling with easy sexual opportunity doesn't necessarily mean you have a disorder. Often, going overboard comes from being new to the apps, and sometimes it's from being newly single or newly coming out. Often, the obsession subsides. And if you take time off from

Grindr or your other favorite app, there's nothing wrong with returning to it, when you feel you're back in control.

But while you are considering what you want to do, be aware of the heterosexism and hidden homophobia that may poison your ideas about sex. Gay apps can become unhealthy, but they open up opportunities for men to connect, and that's healthy. Once, I myself had internalized homophobia about "excessive gay sex." Over time, I've become more sex-positive and gay-affirmative. I don't think we should put a wet blanket over the entire community and say that something's wrong with us for wanting to connect sexually. People say, "Look at the gay men. They're all overly sexual." We buy into that, and we shouldn't.

In the end, you will let the apps serve your needs. I wouldn't rule them out as dating opportunities. A lot of my clients use them that way. Yes, they're mostly for random hookups, but that doesn't mean you can't use them to meet Mr. Right. Keep your boundaries. If you're only on there to meet somebody special, and a contact sends you a dick pic or an ass pic or doesn't listen to you and starts talking sexually, you just need to ignore him and move on. Hold out for the sort of person you're looking for.

Dating When You're Older: Embrace Your Cougay!

As a therapist, I see many gay male clients who are struggling with middle age. As a middle-aged gay man, I understand the struggle. When I was a younger therapist, older gay men in their 40s, 50s and 60s would tell me they disappeared at gay events, and that other gay men—particularly younger ones—didn't notice them. I didn't believe them. I told these men that life is what you make of it, and if they were invisible, we needed to discover what they were doing to make that happen.

As I approached my later 40s, and now in my early 50s, I see exactly what they were talking about. I have literally been standing in a bar behind younger guys who turned around and bumped right into me as if I wasn't there. Heads don't turn toward me the way they did when I was younger. As one ages, one notices these things.

I once told a gay male client in his 20s who was struggling with not feeling attractive that he was, in fact, a very handsome and hot guy, and that we needed to work on his self-esteem. I immediately followed this by reassuring him that I was not coming on to him. He responded, "Why would I ever think you were coming on to me?" That is when I realized he didn't even see me as a sexual being.

American culture worships youth and beauty, and this is even more so in the gay community. Historically when gay men reach a certain age, they tend to withdraw from the dating and bar scene, from interaction with younger men, afraid that they will no longer be seen as attractive, or will be seen as predators.

Unfortunately, the striving for a younger body and stronger libido is leading to an alarming trend I am seeing among middle-aged gay men: The use of crystal meth. This is not the answer. There are far healthier ways to retain a sense of virility, attractiveness and relevance.

To fight the negative feelings of older gay men who want to date, I'm proposing we begin using the word "Cougay," the counterpart of the label given to older women—"cougars"—who have enjoyed the benefits of staying relevant and sexy. Becoming a cougar has been called a source of self-empowerment for women. We gay men are also capable of being vibrant and alive, and remaining attractive and alluring when we are no longer young.

In fact, there's a thing going on now in the gay community. Men 40 and older are being approached by younger guys, usually in their 20s and early 30s, and being identified as "daddies." There are even some websites already established for "daddies" and their admirers, one being www.daddyhunt.com.[6]

But some older gay men don't know how to respond when approached this way. What often happens is that an older man is on Grindr or some other gay app, and suddenly a young guy contacts him, "Hey daddy!" or "Hot daddy!"

I've had gay clients tell me it's offensive. My client Jim felt that way. He was already self-conscious about his age. He was a midlife gay guy, and here's this kid calling him "Daddy." And to top it off—and this is really common—he *was* a father of two teenaged boys. So, to have some young guy contacting him for sex and calling him "Daddy" really creeped him out.

"Look," I told him. "This isn't about being a real daddy. It has nothing to do with incest. They want you to be a 'hot daddy,' but it's mostly just make-believe. These guys are sexualizing you, objectifying you. They're wanting you to enter into their fantasy."

I explained to Jim about the possible benefits of taking on the "Cougay" role, but he was still worried: "This kid wants to be my boy. I just can't deal with that."

"No," I told him, "he wants to be your b – o – i. He wants you to be playful and role-play a daddy-son relationship. There's nothing inherently wrong with this. You don't have to do it, Jim, if you don't want to, but you can also have fun with it. It's an opportunity to play with a younger guy who wants to play with you."

Jim was worried that the young men who approached him would be trying to get money from him. He feared they wanted a sugar daddy; they'd try to make him pay to play. But that's not usually what these guys want. True, these connections are not usually about relationships; the young men are not looking to set up housekeeping with an older guy. On the other hand, often the younger men are looking for more than just a little fun. They want connection and mentoring. They want to be blessed by a father figure.

Jim was also worried that these guys had to be psychologically messed up. "Why would they want this? Something must be wrong with them."

I do have a sense of what's going on, because a number of these young men have been my clients. They either have not been fathered well, so they've sexualized that neglect and are looking for a father figure in the erotic realm. Or they've been so well-fathered that they want more of it. I've seen that side, too.

But while their sexual interests may be the result of childhood experiences, maybe bad experiences, that doesn't mean there's anything wrong with playing with them now. Their past might in reality have been a jungle of pathology, but sexualizing it now makes a garden for play. Yes, if there's a destructive compulsive side, they will need to address that in therapy. Otherwise, it's harmless. And I salute their ability to have their fun. I don't see anything wrong with it.

Personally, I am working on owning the Cougay label. Despite the fact that I have been in a solid relationship for 22 years now, I still want to be seen as vibrant and attractive by others. Don't we all? I am still an individual, and I enjoy flirting and playing with sexual and flirtatious energy. So I work hard to lose the extra weight that age often brings, and I seek out younger people to be a part of my life.

In fact, I suggest that older gay men enjoy the freer sexuality that comes from getting older. Things that you thought you could never do before, or would never have had the nerve to try, you can do now. Try experimenting safely with other sexual ways of being that don't only involve erections. Sex can include fantasy, role-play, and kink.

Claim your Cougay! You're earned the right by suffering the slings and arrows of our heterosexist culture for so many years. It's time to claim the respect (and fun) you deserve.

PART 2: Sexual Hazards

Sexual play and hookups, while fun, can come with a price. You must educate yourself to avoid sexually transmitted infections (STIs). One in four sexually active people get herpes. People are still contracting AIDS. From herpes to AIDS, STIs need to be taken seriously. This book is not the place to learn about them, although I'll touch on a few topics. You can begin online with the CDC's website: www.cdc.gov/std/.[7]

Condoms are the first line of defense, but much progress has been made recently with antiviral medicines. To quote the CDC, "Pre-exposure prophylaxis, or PrEP, is a way for people who do not have HIV but who are at substantial risk of getting it to prevent HIV infection by taking a pill every day. When someone is exposed to HIV through sex or injection drug use, these medicines can work to keep the virus from establishing a permanent infection. When taken consistently, PrEP has been shown to reduce the risk of HIV infection in people who are at high risk by up to 92%. PrEP ... can be combined with condoms and other prevention methods to provide even greater protection than when used alone."

Get the facts, and play safe. When I have a client who is ignoring risks and having unsafe sex, I immediately suspect an underlying psychological cause. Unnecessary risk-taking is one sign of trauma re-enactment leading to problematic sexual behavior, as discussed in the next section.

PART 3. Problematic Sexual Behavior

What Is Problematic and What Is Not?

"Problematic sexual behavior" (PSB) is a *sexual health problem* in which an individual's consensual sexual urges, thoughts, and behaviors lead to troublesome consequences. "Consensual" rules out pedophilia, rape, or other sexual violence. "Sexual health problem" rules out mental illnesses such as bipolar disorder, borderline personality disorder, and various antisocial personality disorders.

Looking at consequences is the only rational way to evaluate how problematic a sexual behavior is. Having strong sexual interests is not necessarily problematic. Neither is having a lot of sex. Neither is having unusual sexual interests and behaviors, as long as nobody gets hurt by them.

Your partner may not be comfortable with your sexual interests, and the consequence is that this may be causing problems in your relationship. However, there may be nothing inherently unhealthy about your sexual interests. You and your partner may just be incompatible as a couple. Should you modify your sexual interests and behaviors to save your relationship? You cannot change your sexual interests. They are inherent. You can always consider changing your behaviors to save your relationship. The devil here is in the details. Sometimes changing is possible and worthwhile; sometimes it isn't. Only you can decide.

There is a lot of talk these days about "sexual addiction," which generally refers to sexual behavior that is difficult to stop despite bad consequences. It is possible for a person to be troubled by "out-of-control sexual behaviors" (OCSB), which is the phrase I prefer to "sexual addiction" (see below). Sometimes, a person's sexual behavior is truly compulsive and difficult to control, despite the consequences. Sometimes, it is "trauma re-enactment" that can be treated by psychotherapy. However, a person can have strong sexual interests which he finds difficult to ignore without there being a problem. A person who really likes something may simply want to do it.

Let me be very clear. Some people really like sex. They have a "high sex drive." When would we (or should they) decide they are engaging in PSB? Put plainly, wanting or having lots of sex is not a disorder, as long as the consequences are not destructive. High-sex-drive people do not necessarily suffer from a psychological problem.

The issue of consequences is many-layered. Legal consequences cannot be ignored. In places where sodomy is illegal, couples engaging in anal sex must consider the trouble they might get into, even though anal sex in itself isn't unhealthy. Social consequences may also be a factor. Being gay is still socially unacceptable in many subcultures of the United States, and being out can have consequences, even though there is nothing wrong with being gay. Personal consequences include risk of disease, spending too much money, spending too much time, or otherwise harming yourself, without directly harming anyone else. It goes without saying that any behavior that harms others is unhealthy and must be stopped. How long should a person be allowed to put only himself at jeopardy before an intervention is called for? This question has no easy answer.

One final point: No matter how unusual a sexual fantasy might be, it is not automatically "problematic." Problems are defined by consequences, and only behaviors have consequences. Yes, individuals, society, the law often define "problematic sex" by type or category, but this is not psychologically justified. Even so, to protect yourself, you should keep in mind that behavior that seems to you to be "obviously innocent" may get you into trouble with your neighbors or the law. After all, until recently (and in many places still today), being gay was a crime.

What Is OCSB?

Therapists Douglas Braun-Harvey and Michael Vigorito[8] use the phrase "out-of-control sexual behavior" (OCSB) to capture the sexual behavioral issues of clients who want to do one thing while doing another and experience a feeling of being out of control as a result. OCSB is offered as an alternative concept to "sexual addiction."

The "sex addict" typically feels out of control, but by not using the language of addictions, the concept of OCSB puts the emphasis on what the individual wants. OCSB does not commit itself to a (rigid) addiction model. It focuses on the point of view of a client who comes to see a therapist with concerns that his sexual behavior is "out of control." (Such clients often come in claiming they are "sex addicts," or at least they fear they are.) The therapist works as a partner with the client to develop a reasonable plan to make things better. OCSB rejects the idea that treatment is being imposed on the client by an outside "authority," as is the case with some "sexual addiction" treatment programs.

OCSB represents a perspective in the therapeutic community to stop being sex-negative, to focus on problems people are actually having and stay away from moral and religious rules and regulations. Being gay isn't bad; masturbating isn't bad; porn isn't bad; BDSM isn't bad. Calling these behaviors "bad" is essentially a moral judgment, and we therapists want to focus on the practical problems people are having, not moral theories.

It is very common for certain types of people to *think* they have OCSB even when an outside observer might not reach that conclusion. By our definition of OCSB, these people do have

OCSB, because their sexual behaviors are troubling them. These individuals are often characterized by their *attitude* toward sexuality. They tend to share some of the following characteristics: They are religious, have negative attitudes about porn, are judgmental about (their own and other people's) sexual morality, are more depressed, have substance abuse problems, are more prone to sexual boredom, and/or have naturally high sex drives. I see in my clients with OCSB significant shame, especially sexual shame. They usually have a lack of accurate sex education and commonly fight their natural sexual desires, especially fetishes and kinks.

My gay clients who are in their "gay adolescence" (Stage Five of coming out; see Chapter 2) are often suffering from OCSB because they are so eager to enjoy their natural gay sexuality after denying it for so long. A male adolescent's inability to control his sexual behavior might be expected because of his adolescent impulse-control issues and the newness of sex for him and his inexperience with it. If an older man is obsessed with sex, then his behavior might lead him to conclude that he has OCSB. However, newly out gay men will often focus excessively on sex, even if they are older. Gay adolescence usually transitions into more mature sexual behavior within a few years.

Your sexual behavior is "out of control" only if you decide it is. No one else has the right to decide this for you. Again, getting into trouble around sex doesn't necessarily mean you are at fault. The trouble might be circumstantial, not inherent. It could be grounded in religion, culture, or the tastes of the people around you. Any of these things can create conflict for you, but it doesn't mean there's something wrong with you.

On the other hand, if you are constantly putting yourself at risk with your sexual behavior, regret it but can't seem to stop, then you may indeed have a problem. I discuss the underlying psychological processes for this kind of behavior in Chapter 7 of my book *10 Smart Things Gay Men Can Do to Find Real Love*. Generally, it is wise to seek the advice of a therapist who specializes in treating sexual problems; i.e., a certified sex therapist.

I recently had a client, Colin, who came to consult with me about his "sexual addiction." He was ashamed because he enjoyed what he called "compulsive masturbation" and looking at pornography of men with big penises. He had been working with a series of therapists who told him in no uncertain terms that his masturbation was compulsive. They said that he ought to want to express his sexuality in a loving committed relationship. He wasn't in such a relationship (they said) because of his "addiction." His therapists had recommended 12-step groups for sex addicts, and he had dutifully attended these groups.

When I asked him if being in a loving, committed relationship was what he wanted, he responded, "Shouldn't that be what I want?" I replied that he should want whatever *he* wanted. He had a full social life and very close friends. He had a prior partner of 10 years whom he loved, but it didn't work out, though they remained friends. He was neither yearning for another partner nor excluding the possibility. I asked him to consider whether masturbation and fantasy were actually what he wanted.

As a strict sex-addiction therapist, I would have pushed Colin to wonder why he was "avoiding" relationships, and I would have attempted to convince him that his compulsive masturbation was interfering with his life. I would have directed him to 12-step programs to stop the masturbation, to work on dating and finding himself a partner.

I would have examined his childhood with him for sexual, physical, and emotional abuse. Anything we found would have been explored as possibly contributing to his "addiction." We would have come up with nonsexual ways he could self-soothe himself to make it easier for him to give up masturbation. If Colin had continued to masturbate, in my role as a sex-addiction therapist I would have been forced to conclude that he was "slipping" and "relapsing" and never "recovering" until he stopped.

However, my approach to help Colin was different from this. I examined with him—from his point of view and values—whether or not *he* felt his sexual behavior was compulsive and interfering in his life. In fact, he told me that he enjoyed what he was doing. He was open to the possibility that someday someone special might come along, but a relationship was not high on his list of needs. He had assumed it should be, because that's what his sex-addiction therapists had told him.

Colin and I did talk about his past to see what parts might be driving how he expressed his sexuality, not assuming we'd find something pathological, but rather just for understanding. Using the perspective of OCSB, even if Colin's masturbation and porn use could have been linked to childhood neglect or abuse, I still would not have labeled his sexual behavior a problem unless he thought it was one himself.

I encouraged him to let go of any shame that he had about how he enjoyed himself. I didn't say he had to be in a relationship. I didn't try to move him in any particular direction. This was very different from my training as a sexual addiction therapist in which I was taught to push the client toward "relational sexual health."

All of us have threads from our childhood that influence our sexual desires, fantasies and behaviors. You have an opportunity to learn to play with your sexuality and claim it as your own rather than fighting it throughout your life.

Confusing Fetishes with Compulsive Sexual Behavior

"I keep going back to this same thing over and over again. I try to stop, but I can't stop. I can't control it." This is what might be called a compulsion: An interest or behavior with failed attempts to stop, spending more and more amounts of time engaged with it, wanting it more and more. But this pattern also captures any hobby or profession that becomes more and more engrossing, from watching football to playing video games. Many of the young scientists and engineers I've interviewed have been utterly consumed by their profession, spending almost all their time on it, often neglecting other important things in their lives.

But sex is less respectable in our society than science or engineering.

Expressing your natural sexuality is not necessarily unhealthy, and "trying to stop" something so fundamental to your nature is bound to fail. As the late psychologist Jack Morin famously summarized, "If you go to war with your sexuality, you will lose, and end up in more trouble than before you started."[9] Fetishes can feel especially like compulsions, their pull is so strong. But most fetishes are harmless. The harm comes from fighting your own sexual nature. If you are at odds with your sexuality, fighting it will contribute to your grief around it.

You may be turned on by spanking, and spending too much time and money on your computer with spanking porn. The problem is not the fact that you are turned on by spanking, which you cannot change. The problem is the time and money that you need to manage more effectively. If you are struggling with a psychological compulsion—perhaps you are re-enacting childhood trauma—then you may need therapy to give you control over the compulsion. But being turned on by spanking is inherent to your sexuality. When you have successfully completed therapy and can now manage your time and money, spanking will still turn you on. This remains true even if you never look at porn again. A celibate priest is still a sexual person, merely one who has chosen to not act with respect to his sexuality.

Some "authorities" and leaders of the sexual addiction community have an extreme overreaction to fetishes. They say things like "All violence is bad and must be stopped" in response to the mildest forms of BDSM play. I take the position that nonstandard sexual tastes are not necessarily bad. Men are especially likely to have fetishes (twenty times more likely than women). How you're wired, what you're into … it may be nonstandard but it's not necessarily "bad."

Childhood Sexual Abuse

What is the nature of childhood sexual abuse? Abuse occurs when an adult dominates and exploits a child—thereby violating trust and the promise of protection. Abuse can occur in any relationship with a power differential. The abuser uses his superior position to manipulate, misuse, degrade, humiliate, or even hurt another—who, by inference, is always inferior. Many studies have confirmed that the basic motivation for rape is power, not sex. Other forms of sexual abuse follow the same pathology.

The sexual abuser's ideal target is a child who's still naive, lacking the "immune system" imparted by emotional and intellectual experience that tells him when he's being violated— and when to resist, and when to say no. A dominant perpetrator— uncle, stepfather, or other male figure who's familiar, trusted, and seems all-powerful—can easily lure a boy into a sexual relationship and force him to comply.

There are several important points to make about the consequences of childhood sexual abuse.

First, childhood sexual abuse can be a significant trauma that a person carries as a heavy burden into adulthood. An abused person may have a compulsion to act out sexual scripts that reflect the abuse, even if he has "forgotten" that he was abused. This unconscious process is sometimes summarized as "turning trauma into orgasm." Until the source of the trauma is resolved, the sexual re-enactments never end. In other words, unresolved childhood sexual abuse can lead to compulsive sexual behaviors. The adult abused as a child often requires psychotherapy to break the control that the compulsion has over his life.

Second, when a man abuses a boy who is straight, the boy sometimes grows up to feel a compulsion to have sex with men, even though he is not gay or bisexual. I discuss this situation at length in my book *Is My Husband Gay, Straight, or Bi?*[10] When the trauma of the abuse is resolved in therapy, the straight man is no longer drawn to sex with men. He was not gay or bisexual. Being abused cannot change a straight boy's orientation, but when the straight man is drawn to want sex with men, he is often confused and thinks he may be gay or bi. I say: Sexual abuse can disorient you, but it cannot orient you.

Third, a boy who is gay may be damaged by abuse. When the abused boy grows up, the gay man must deal both with the trauma-induced compulsion to act out sexually with men and also his own gay sexual nature. This confusion can significantly prolong his coming-out process.

Therapy is generally required to resolve the trauma of sexual abuse, whether the man is gay, bi, or straight. Many men who come to my office for treatment of PSB learn that the origin of their compulsion is in childhood sexual abuse. Whether he is gay, bi, or straight, the man has been damaged by the trauma of the abuse, but his inherent orientation has not been changed by it.

We gay men are taught early on not to be intimate with each other, let alone be open to our families or classmates. Abuse that begins early in a gay boy's life leaves him extremely susceptible to intimacy issues.

Sexual abuse can shape your fantasies, but that's not necessarily something you have to change. A client of mine suffered sexual abuse when he was a child. He had been perpetrated by his best friend's father. The man was significantly hairy, and as a direct result of the abuse, my client was into hairy guys. And that's okay. Yes, the father of his best friend should never have abused him, and there were negative consequences that my client had to deal with in therapy. But being into hairy guys was not one of the consequences that needed to be changed.

One final point: There's a body of published research that shows "abused" and "traumatized" don't always go together.[11] Not everyone who has been sexually abused is traumatized by the abuse. I'm not saying, of course, that abuse is a good thing, only that people differ in the damage they experience from potentially traumatic events. Abuse might affect your sexual taste and at the same time not drive your behavior. But taste doesn't require therapy; only behavior does.

Some gay men have told me that they enjoyed parts of their childhood sexual abuse with adult men. They say, "This was my first sexual experience, and I enjoyed it." Early in my career, I was very surprised and in disbelief. I spent many years confronting my gay clients when they said this. I insisted that they couldn't have enjoyed it, because it was all bad and all abuse. Over time, I've learned from my clients and my training that there are parts of childhood sexual abuse that people sometimes enjoy, and I cannot take that away from them. So, I've moderated my response to my clients who say this, and I'm telling you, my reader, because I want you not to feel ashamed if you reflect back on your childhood sexual abuse and say, "You know, there were parts of it I liked." That's normal. It's okay. It makes sense. It doesn't mean that you liked the abuse. It means that parts of the abuse were your first sexual experience.

The Story of Walt: A Gay Boy Abused

Walt (a gay man) was arrested for public indecency after flashing an undercover police officer in a public restroom. In therapy, he told me that he had been doing this throughout his adult life. He also disclosed that he wasn't happy with his partner.

Even though he was in a committed relationship, Walt had frequented rest areas and restrooms in malls and airports without his partner, Zack, knowing about it. Because he preferred cruising to spending time with Zack, he assumed their relationship was over.

During our work together, I suggested that his sexual behavior in public might be the root of his problem, and his relationship with Zack might be salvageable. Despite his unhappiness, Walt defended his compulsive sexual behavior. He enjoyed the risk, as well as the novelty, of sex with the new men he met.

In exploring his childhood, Walt recalled his grandfather giving him a bath at the age of six. The grandfather washed Walt's penis and scrotum for an unusually long time. Finally, Walt asked, "Why are you doing that?" His grandfather said his penis was dirty and needed extra attention. Walt dried off, dressed, and went downstairs to tell his grandmother, who dismissed the whole issue. Walt never tried to discuss the incident with his parents at all, but he knew something was wrong. His mother had never washed him that way. His grandfather had done something bad to him. Walt didn't know what it was called; at six years old, he didn't have the concepts or vocabulary to talk about being sexually groped. But what his grandfather had done bothered him at the time, until he "forgot" about it.

He was left without any resolution. He had needed validation: someone to tell him that his grandfather had done wrong and that Walt had done the right thing when he told his grandmother about it. His grandfather should have felt fear, shame, and anxiety about what he had done. Instead, Walt took those emotions on himself and lived with them.

After he grew up, he frequented public bathrooms and rest areas. He jerked off with strangers and enjoyed oral sex through glory holes. Only quick anonymous sex interested him. He didn't want to meet men online, in bars, or in clubs.

I helped him understand the connection: His grandfather had molested him in a bathroom. Now, his unconscious—having received no resolution to the trauma—was "telling about it" through his compulsive sexual behavior in bathrooms.

Walt eventually told Zack about his arrest and about what he had learned in therapy. Zack tried to help Walt by being creative. They put up a drywall "stall," drilled a glory hole, and engaged in oral sex. For a while, this private glory hole—and the legal charges hanging over his head—helped Walt resist his urge to cruise. He and Zack began to work on their relationship with me, while Walt explored his compulsive sexual behavior.

But he didn't want to look very closely at what his grandfather had done, other than to accept that it happened and that it was linked to his public sexual behavior. He wanted to "move on." I strongly encouraged him to look at the abuse more closely to help resolve it.

I was running a group for men who'd been sexually abused and who were having problems with sex. Walt declined to join the group, saying that individual therapy and periodic couples therapy with Zack were enough. Walt had stopped seeking sex in public bathrooms, and he now felt that he had been "cured."

But after a while, the glory hole in his basement no longer gave him enough pleasure. After his legal hassles cleared, his urge for bathroom sex returned. He told me that despite the risk, he wanted to keep on cruising rest areas and bathrooms, because, "It brings me joy."

When he finally agreed to join the group, Walt responded to my challenges and admitted he was in total relapse. He began working harder on his recovery and his relationship. Ultimately, he became internally motivated. He could take charge of his life without needing the external threat of possible legal consequences.

Summary: Sexual Health, Hazards, and Problems

As a gay man, you have choices in how you express your sexuality. No one should tell you what you ought to like. Anal sex? Open relationships? Yes, if you want it; no, if you don't. Go slow if that's what you want. Enjoy hookups if that's what you want, as long as you play safely. See what works for you.

Don't stop yourself from being sexually free. We do not need to feel morally bound by the sex-negativity of heterosexist culture. I love the idea and reality of homoflexible gays who are having sex with women. Why not, if they enjoy it?

The story of Alan and Brad is about negotiating with your partner. You can work through even the complications of open relationships, if you maintain honest communication and maybe get some support from the occasional helpful therapist.

The actress and performer Cher was interviewed a few years ago and was asked when she would retire, given that there were newer and younger divas coming up behind her. She said that in the old days the older divas got out of the way and made room for the younger ones, and that she had no intention of doing this. She said they would have to go around her! I loved it. I feel the same way as a middle-aged gay man.

Remember, there is a place for us at middle age. Embrace your Daddy! Embrace your Cougay!

Take STIs seriously. If you find yourself engaging in behavior you know is risky but that you feel compelled to do, consider therapy. There might be an underlying psychological cause, and its resolution would allow you to take better care of yourself.

The issue of problematic sexual behavior is very complex. Behavior can be a problem even if it isn't unhealthy. You must be aware of societal and legal consequences, as well as consequences to yourself and the people you love. If you find yourself endangering yourself, spending too much time and money on sex and porn, engaging in damaging activities and unable to stop in spite of the consequences, then you may need help to address what you are doing and regain control over your behaviors. Be aware that compulsions often have a psychological basis; a good therapist can help you discover what's going on.

But having strong sexual interests is not necessarily unhealthy, not necessarily problematic, not necessarily compulsive. Decide if you have a problem by the consequences of your behavior, not by the content of your fantasies. Get help if you need it. Otherwise, enjoy!

A man who was abused as a child can be strongly affected by that experience. He may find his life ruled by sexual compulsions. He may be significantly confused about his orientation. But don't forget that sexual abuse disorients you; it does not orient you. This is my most important point. When you deal with the trauma of the abuse, the confusion, the "disorientation," is lifted, and you can discover your true orientation. Your sexual preferences may be permanently affected by the abuse, but you can still regain control over your sexual behavior, even if that's been a problem, through therapy.

References

1. Joe Kort. "Guys on the 'Side': Looking Beyond Gay Tops and Bottoms," *Huffington Post*, April 16, 2013.

2. Michael C. LaSala. "Monogamous or Not: Understanding and Counseling Gay Male Couples," *Families in Society*, Vol. 82 (6), 2000.
3. Joe Kort. *10 Smart Things Gay Men Can Do to Find Real Love*. New York: Alyson Books, 2003.
4. Tristan Taormino. *Opening Up: A Guide to Creating and Sustaining Open Relationships*. Berkeley, California: Cleis Press, 2008.
5. Helen Fisher. *Anatomy of Love: A Natural History of Mating, Marriage, and Why We Stray*, revised edition. New York: W. W. Norton & Company, 2016.
6. www.daddyhunt.com
7. www.cdc.gov/std/
8. Douglas Braun-Harvey and Michael Vigorito. *Treating Out of Control Sexual Behavior: Rethinking Sex Addiction*. New York: Springer, 2015.
9. Jack Morin. *The Erotic Mind: Unlocking the Inner Sources of Sexual Passion and Fulfillment*. Harper Perennial, 1996.
10. Joe Kort with Alexander P. Morgan. *Is My Husband Gay, Straight, or Bi: A Guide for Women Concerned about Their Men*. Lanham, Maryland: Rowman & Littlefield, 2014.
11. Susan A. Clancy. *The Trauma Myth: The Truth About the Sexual Abuse of Children—and Its Aftermath*. New York: Basic Books, 2011.

Chapter 6

Learn from Mentors, Then Become One

Gay, schmay! Just don't be alone.

—My Grandmother

Most of what I know of Jewish tradition was passed to me by my grandmother, my *bubbie*. Though not formally educated, she knew quite a bit of Jewish religion and culture, which guided her through her long life.

As I write this, I'm reminded that she insisted that I use her name in print. "Yusella [Yiddish for "Joey" or "little Joe"], when you mention me in your articles, I notice you don't say my name. Why not?"

"Bubbie," I replied, "I didn't know you *had* a name until I was in my teens. Everyone called you Bubbie. Even your friends!"

Mary helped my mother raise me and taught me why we Jews light candles on the Sabbath and keep kosher. (As a child, I was upset that she'd never know the taste of a cheeseburger or pizza with pepperoni.) A woman full of old-world family values, morality, spirituality, and holiness, she was filled with joy whenever she reconnected with her heritage. I relish her stories about coming to America from Russia—and I videotaped her so that I will never forget her words, inflections, and personality.

Unfortunately, she taught me not only spirituality but superstition. Even today, when I spill salt accidentally, I automatically shake it over my shoulder three times.

I'll always have memories of this strong matriarch who taught me the Jewish way. "Just don't be alone" was her way of blessing me personally, as being both Jewish and gay.

At age 13, I had my Bar Mitzvah. As the joke goes, "Today, I'm a man. Tomorrow, eighth grade!" Though really still a boy, I was initiated into manhood through prayer and celebration.

Young Gay Men Need "Gay Tribal Elders"

As gay men, we don't often receive other people's blessings. Very few mentors come forward to guide LGBTQ youth. A lesbian comic once joked that as a girl, her role models were Dr. Smith on *Lost In Space* and Ms. Hathaway on *The Beverly Hillbillies*. What kind of role models are they?

I always felt grief when I was younger and an older man asked me (because I was out) what gay culture was like. It should have been the other way around; he should have been mentoring me! In LGBTQ culture, our identity is formed in adulthood, and we must mentor each other and ourselves.

Some very wonderful things characterize gay culture.

One: We're not bound by gender roles. When we're partnered, stereotypical expectations don't exist. Everything has to be negotiated—just as it must be in any relationship. We get to decide what works best for us.

Most male partners have been groomed to be breadwinners and providers. So who vacuums and who takes out the garbage? Partnered women have been raised to nurture and make a home. At least one woman in a lesbian couple has to go out and work.

Two: We tend to explore and examine our sexuality more openly than heterosexuals. Heterosexism and homophobia have forced us to talk about our sexuality and develop a language for it. Many heterosexuals, both male and female, have difficulty knowing what they want, let alone talking about their desires.

Three: Gay culture is very honest. I think our best features are courage, assertiveness, and affirmation. It takes bravery and sincerity to come out of the closet in a society that would rather we stay hidden.

When we are honest enough to come out, others become honest with us as well. It forces truth to the forefront for all. In the movie *In and Out*, Kevin Kline portrays a gay man. In one scene, his mother tells her girlfriends her son is gay. At that, her girlfriends decide to take risks, be honest with each other, and "come out" about their own deep, dark secrets. It illustrates what happens when we—and those around us—really tell the truth

Unfortunately, a gay man's initiation into manhood is usually purely sexual. Society doesn't approve of an older gay man's nonsexual contact with a younger boy or teen, because people assume that *sexual* contact is all the elder wants. So when a young gay man reaches his 20s, his initiation into gay culture is often through sexuality—in relation to a "mentor" he'll probably never see again. This young gay man—just coming out and not sure of himself—hasn't learned it's okay to approach a gay man nonsexually. So he goes the sexual, secretive, anonymous route—to the Internet, gay apps, or gay bars. If older and younger gay men could gather in groups and sit down for tea and coffee, how different things would be.

In *Gay Spirit Warrior: An Empowerment Workbook for Men Who Love Men*, John Stowe writes, "Imagine a society different from our own, in which older gay men are treated with honor. Imagine a Council of Gay Elders who sit together in order to share wisdom and advice with the entire Tribe. Imagine going to this Council—being sent by your parents, even—the moment you first recognized your attraction to other men. Imagine sharing your concerns with a silver-haired mentor, a man like yourself who loves other men and who listens to you with respect. Imagine how you'd feel about yourself if you could call on this man's guidance, insight, humor and perspective whenever you need it."[1]

I want to help something like this happen. Society may not give us permission, but you can always give yourself permission.

Care, love, and wisdom are formed in us by the time we reach middle age. Then, we want to share what we have learned with younger generations. In his book *Childhood and Society*, Erik Eriksson says, "Mature man needs to be needed, and maturity needs guidance as well as encouragement from what has been produced and must be taken care of. Generativity, then, is primarily the concern in establishing and guiding the next generation."[2] Younger people need guidance and mentoring, and older people want to mentor. It's human nature, and psychologically necessary.

Jennifer, a heterosexual therapist, had a gay client, Shawn, age 17. I volunteered to come to one of their sessions to let him meet a gay male adult.

Shawn, intelligent and attractive, was just starting to come out. He was scared and lonely. "Where can I find other guys my age?" he asked. "Should I tell my family and friends?" I answered his questions as best I could. A senior in high school, he was very cautious. Ultimately, Shawn told his mother, his father, and a few selected friends and teachers.

Months later, the Human Rights Campaign held its annual fundraising dinner. At the event members of our community receive awards for their work, locally and nationally, to advance the cause of equal rights for LGBTQ individuals.

My husband and I had already paid to go, but I received some free tickets. I called Jennifer and asked her permission to invite Shawn and his family. I wanted him to have a positive, healthy experience in the gay community. Jennifer thought that was a great idea!

Shawn and his parents were thankful and honored to sit at the same table with my husband and me, along with several of our friends, both coupled and single. I was so proud to be able to show Shawn some solid role models—and show his family what gays and lesbians could achieve. Shawn's mother knew one of the award recipients and spoke to her at length about mothering a gay son.

The night was a success. One of my friends at the table made friends with Shawn and his parents. Later, he went to lunch with them and told me that he, too, wanted to help mentor this young man and his family.

I haven't been exempt from wanting a gay mentor. I've always been a fan of Brian McNaught, whose many books include *On Being Gay*[3] (chapters were written and published as articles in 1975!), *Gays In The Workplace*,[4] and *Now That I'm Out, What Do I Do?*[5] He's a Detroit native, widely respected here and around the country. A few years ago, my husband, Mike, and I were on vacation in Provincetown when I spotted McNaught. I felt like a fan after a rock star's autograph!

Anxious and overwhelmed, I asked Mike what to do. Even Oprah talks about how we should take a moment to thank the person who's been a role model and paved the way for our journeys. Finally, I decided to approach Brian and tell him how much he'd meant to me and that his work inspired my own. He was very gracious, gave me his card, and told me to keep in touch.

I was elated. On returning home, I sent him a few of my writings. He responded with a handwritten note saying that he'd read each of my articles and enjoyed them. That meant so much to me—and I feel I am standing on his shoulders today.

My friend Steve, who's in his 70s, was partnered for over 20 years until his partner died. Steve is a vessel of wisdom about the joys and challenges of gay relationships. I still do what's right for me, of course, but I need Steve's "elder" opinion and I'm grateful for it.

Accept The Challenge of Being a "Gay Tribal Elder"

I talked in Chapter 5 about the struggle older gay men have keeping their sense of virility, attractiveness and relevance. Recognizing your value and worth as a gay mentor can help give you perspective on your value and worth as an older gay man. Believing that you must be at your peak of youth and hotness to be valued in the gay community is a dangerous trap that can end in many forms of tragedy, from drug addiction to isolation to severe depression.

Perhaps one of the saddest examples of gay middle-aged self-loathing was the Manhattan therapist Bob Bergeron. A handsome, successful man, Bergeron was weeks away from having his book, *The Right Side of Forty: The Complete Guide to Happiness for Gay Men at Midlife and Beyond,*[6] published. As a man approaching middle age myself, I looked forward to the book. I had watched his videos and wanted to learn what more someone in my own field and dealing with own my impending issues could teach me.

Then he committed suicide. I was horrified. Apparently, Bergeron found the prospect of becoming middle-aged unbearable.

This is exactly what should not happen. Separation of old and young in our society is increasingly understood as undesirable and unhealthy, leading to isolation and to the detriment of both groups. Due to the devastation that AIDS wreaked in the gay community in decades past, there is a notable lack of older gay role models from whom younger men—and other middle-aged men—might benefit from knowing and interacting with.

I challenge my clients to work on staying in shape through exercise and eating well, but also to remain involved in the gay social scene, to be out among younger people. Many people have noted that having younger friends makes one feel younger. And if they are rejected or made to feel invisible, I encourage them not to take it personally, not to neuter themselves or give up on their sexuality, and not to be offended by younger guys who might call them "Daddy."

I challenge them to keep dating, even though it gets harder when you are older, especially in the gay male community. This calls for consistently changing your dating strategies, as well as your expectations. For instance, in dating it is important to notice how you are dressing. You don't have to be making a fashion statement, but keeping up with various clothing options that make you feel better about yourself keeps you confident, and other gay men will see this.

So, embrace being a Daddy or a Cougay or a Gay Elder! It's a big world out there, and someone will find you attractive, your accumulated experience valuable, and your personality charming. Having father energy and playing with it can be very fun. I have always been drawn to paternal men and have had a need for their blessings. Now, as an older man, I enjoy offering younger gay men the blessings derived from the wisdom I've gained over the years. I am energized by the things I can say and do to help them feel better and more confident about themselves.

Men Have Trouble Trusting One Another

Older and younger gay men are deeply suspicious of one another. Older men fear younger men just want "daddies" to take care of them. Typically, they misinterpret a younger gay man's "neediness" and worry about being used, and therefore disregard these younger men, which makes their own loneliness more acute.

Older gay men tell me about feeling unwanted, and hold ageism accountable for how they're treated. Several older gay clients have told me they feel that younger men look right through them. (Heterosexual older women have reported the same experience.) Men in general prize youth and beauty in their partners.

Many younger gay men are lonely, long for male recognition, and sometimes use sexuality to get their elders' attention. Again, this is a result of our community's not having a built-in mentor system. One client in his 20s told me he enjoyed talking to older gays but felt awkward nonetheless. He tried to keep a distance— even when he wanted to get to know them better—because they usually interpreted his friendliness as an interest in sex.

Trust is essential in mentoring, but trust is rare in the gay community. Trust of other men is low among men in general. Many straight women I know talk about not trusting the men who pay attention to them. Most of the attention they've received has been sexual, so they hold men suspect. Straight men usually don't have to worry about that from other men. But they do harbor a general distrust for one another, regardless of age and orientation.

A lot of straight men I treat didn't get blessings from their fathers or other men in their lives. They feel deeply wounded and starved for affirmations. They are not gay or bisexual—they just need healthy role models. Through therapy, I become a mentor for them or help them find other men in their lives to help make them stronger.

The same is true for gay men, only more so. In his popular and widely respected book, *Being Homosexual: Gay Men and Their Development*, Richard Isay states: "If the fathers of homosexual boys were accepting and loving toward them, these children would have a model for loving and caring for other men, a model that has not been traditionally available in our society. Fathers who nurture the development of their homosexual sons, who affirm their worth by giving of their time and attention, encouraging and supporting their son's interests, and who are not dismissive or censorious will help their sons to be capable, as gay adults, of loving, affectionate, and sexually responsive lasting relationships."[7] I believe Isay speaks for all men—gay, bisexual, and straight. If all fathers demonstrated the role model that Isay discusses, heterosexual men could have trusting, solid, and supportive relationships with other men. Gay and bisexual men could have the same, along with healthy sexual/romantic relationships.

I tell older clients who wish to mentor, befriend, or date younger gay men to keep themselves out there—available and visible. Lots of younger men want and need the advice, strength, and friendship of a gay elder. And they may want to date and have a relationship.

At one of my workshops for gay men, a 25-year-old named Robb approached me. He felt uncomfortable around another workshop participant—Greg, 60, who'd been out all his life. Robb was just coming out, was new to coming to gay events, and feared Greg wanted to prey on him sexually.

"Why do you think Greg is coming on to you?" I asked. Robb said it was the way Greg looked at him and the things he said. Greg had told Robb about his own coming out, 40 years before, and how different things were today. Greg complimented Robb on his bravery, told him he was a very good-looking and charming, and asked Robb to go out for a coffee some time. Greg hugged Robb to welcome him into the workshop and the gay community. Robb felt that he was trying to create a romantic and sexual relationship.

At my workshops, participants have opportunities to resolve conflicts with others. I told Robb that I'd invite him to talk to Greg, and I'd help.

After they learned the communication process, Robb asked whether Greg was open to hearing his concerns—to which Greg agreed. Robb explained all that he had told me: that he was uncomfortable, frustrated, and angry because he felt Greg was coming on to him.

When Robb finished, it was Greg's turn to respond. He was shocked by Robb's judgments and reactions. Greg had never thought for a minute about pursuing Robb sexually or romantically. Greg recalled feeling alone and lacking guidance from men in the gay community when he was a young man. He wanted to offer Robb a different experience, and that was all.

Robb began to cry. He said he appreciated what Greg was doing and was sorry he'd misunderstood. Robb had gone to various gay bars and used gay apps where older men had preyed on him, and he thought Greg was doing the same. Both men began to weep. In fact, there wasn't a dry eye in the room.

We Also Need to Be Mentored in Adult Love Relationships

Richard Isay affirms, "Gay men also long to satisfy a desire for closeness to their father that has so often been thwarted or frustrated in childhood. This longing is obvious in the young man looking for an older partner, but it is also seen in the older man who treats his youthful lover with kindness and care and, identifying with him, gets the love that he longs for himself."[8]

This phenomenon mirrors heterosexual men and women who try to meet their emotional needs through older and younger partners. It is unrelated to sexual and romantic orientation but finds its roots in unmet needs from childhood. Relationships are a way to heal and work through those early needs—as we'll consider further in the last three chapters.

Also important is the need to be mentored by witnessing other successful gay relationships. For my husband and me, it's been extremely nourishing to be close friends with a number of other gay male couples. Watching heterosexual couples can also offer insights into standard relationship strategies like anger management, conflict resolution, and open communication (to name just a few).

Straight partners must address their gender differences. Gay men must address the unique things about a male-male relationship: sexual gratification, competitiveness, empathy skills, and other challenging social and genetic traits. The only way to get that form of mentoring is either from another male couple or from a man who's been in healthy gay relationships.

Finding a Mentor/Being a Mentor

My suggestions for finding a mentor:

1. Overcome your anxieties and speak directly to a gay man you admire. He can be chronologically older or in a more mature place in his gay life. Let him know that you appreciate where he is in his life and that you would like to talk to him about what has worked for him and what hasn't. "I enjoy hearing your stories about your life as a gay man. Would you be willing to go for a coffee and share more?"

2. If a man comes on to you, and you aren't interested, tell him. This can be done in a polite, respectful way. Let him know you enjoy his company, but you aren't interested in a romantic and sexual relationship. To honor his feelings, you can ask him, "Will that work for you?"

My suggestions for older men who want to mentor:

1. Don't stay away from certain gay events just because you think you are "too old." Yes, some men there will think you are, but others will be glad to see you. Remember that many younger gay men are starved for role models and mature relationships.

2. If you see a young man you'd like to meet, tell him you think he has a lot going for him and you'd like to get to know him better. If he seems apprehensive, tell him you are not interested in being sexual and that you are genuinely interested in him as a person. If he doesn't believe you and nothing comes of it, don't take it personally. This isn't about you. You've done the right thing for yourself by offering the possibility of a mentoring friendship. You might have negative feelings about the rejection— that is normal. Healthy self-talk might be, "That man has his own reasons for not wanting advice and counsel from me. This isn't about me as a gay man or a person."

3. Go to your local gay community center and let them know you want to be a gay elder and/or gay mentor. If they don't have a program like this available, tell them you'd like to start one.

In *Golden Men: The Power of Gay Midlife*, Harold Kooden and Charles Flowers write, "Our middle years will become golden only if we treat ourselves as if we were carved from real gold: precious, sexy, infinitely malleable, and priceless."[9] I want midlife elders to adopt this attitude. Go into the gay community and see yourself as the priceless asset you are.

References

1. John R. Stowe. *Gay Spirit Warrior: An Empowerment Workbook for Men Who Love Men*. Tallahassee, Florida: Findhorn Press, 1999.
2. Erik Erikson. *Childhood and Society*. New York: W.W. Norton and Company, 1963.
3. Brian McNaught. *On Being Gay: Thoughts on Family, Faith, and Love*. New York: St. Martin's Press, 1983.
4. Brian McNaught. *Gay Issues in the Workplace*. New York: St. Martin's Press, 1993.
5. Brian McNaught. *Now That I'm Out, What Do I Do?* New York: St. Martin's Press, 1997.

6. Bob Bergeron. *Right Side of Forty: The Complete Guide to Happiness for Gay Men at Midlife and Beyond*. New York: Magnus Books, 2012.
7. Richard Isay. *Being Homosexual: Gay Men and Their Development*. The Master Work Series, Softcover Edition, New Jersey: Jason Aronson, 1994.
8. Richard Isay. *Becoming Gay: The Journey to Self-Acceptance*. New York: Pantheon Books, 1996.
9. Harold Kooden with Charles Flowers. *Golden Men: The Power of Gay Midlife*. New York: Avon Books, 2000.

Chapter 7

Take Advantage of Therapy "Workouts"

We see the world as we are, not as it is.

—The Talmud

Thousands of gay men harbor misgivings about entering therapy. They fear hiring a therapist who won't be objective. Many of them seek gay or lesbian therapists, but this isn't necessarily the best step. Working with a gay therapist offers no guarantee that you won't still receive doses of homonegativity and heterosexism. (*Homonegativity* is a lesser form of homophobia. The gay or lesbian person may feel good about being gay but still cultivate negative thoughts about gay culture in general.)

I use an LGBTQ Affirmative psychotherapeutic approach, which addresses the severe psychological consequences of homophobia and heterosexism in childhood and later. It stresses that the problem isn't with the gay individual but with what's been done to that person. When a gay man comes out of the closet, he loses many of the protections and privileges heterosexual males take for granted—and his grief over this loss is often profound.

Dan, My "Ex-Gay" Client

Dan, a 32-year-old single man, heard that I specialize in sexual issues and came to me for help for what he called his "sexual addiction." He was soft-spoken, with a strong tendency toward passivity. He simply responded to events in life rather than taking charge of his own destiny. He was an active member of a church-related organization that focused on "healing homosexuality." The sexual behavior he was worried about—his "sexual addiction"—was that he liked to masturbate while imagining "homosexual" fantasies. (I'm putting *homosexual* in quotes because he used this adjective. For him, it was pejorative. He had been taught not to call it gay, because "there's nothing gay about being homosexual.")

During our evaluation appointment, he told me he was an "ex-gay man" and that he wanted to stay that way. Dan also admitted that he had no sexual interest in women. All his sexual and romantic urges were directed toward adult males. His life goal was to become a celibate monk in the Roman Catholic Church. Thus, any masturbation was deeply troubling to him, and he was depressed about not being able to stop.

He described gay men as "homosexuals," followers of "the alternative lifestyle." He thought that his own homosexual urges were the result of poor, inappropriate fathering. As I've noted in earlier chapters, these are the teachings of "reparative therapies," which have been thoroughly repudiated by the professional psychological community. I told him I was gay and—given how he felt about homosexuality—that he should be aware before he and I entered into therapy that I disagreed with the views of reparative therapy.

To my surprise, he said that my views wouldn't bother him. He didn't feel my beliefs would interfere with my ability to help his "sexually compulsive behaviors." He did want assurance that I wouldn't try to convince him that being gay was the answer to his problems, and I assured him that I wouldn't. My job is to help clients identify what's right for them. But to be honest, I told him that most likely his "masturbatory slips with homosexual imagery" resulted from his attempt to suppress something natural to him. Dan didn't agree with this, but he remained eager to begin therapy.

In my office, I keep a photograph of my husband, Mike, and me, along with pictures of my young nephews and my sister. Dan asked, "Are you happy with your husband?" I answered, "Yes, very happy." He doubted that any gay man could be happy in an "incomplete" partnership, lacking the "complementary female element" (in the words of his reparative therapy group).

I encouraged Dan to talk more about how he felt about me— and my being gay—thus inviting the process of transference, which I explained in Chapter 1. Dan had already begun transferring his negative feelings about his own homosexuality onto me. This was a positive sign that his therapy had let him understand himself. During our sessions, he referred to homosexuality as a "sad lifestyle." He thought I was not truly happy, that I had convinced myself otherwise, and that I was "giving in" to my homosexual urges. He stayed in therapy for approximately eight months, then cancelled an appointment and never returned.

For his own personal and religious reasons, Dan couldn't come to terms with his gayness. I respected his decision to refrain from acting on his homosexual urges, because that's what he wanted to do. But I did question his efforts to deny them and "repair" them. That struggle caused him more depression and difficulty than if he'd just accepted that he was a gay man who'd vowed to live a celibate life.

Keeping one's urges "dirty" and taboo only makes them stronger. When Dan said I was giving in to my homosexuality— something not in my best interest—he was projecting his struggle onto me. In reality, Dan was fooling himself to think he could suppress his own homosexual urges; in fact, he was "giving in" to religion and anti-gay therapies that said there was something wrong with him.

God Wants You to "Act Masculine"

Most religious institutions spurn gay men. Rejected by their clergy, ostracized and outcast from their houses of worship, these gay men often try to replace religion with therapy. I've had many gay Catholic clients who probably would never have come to me if they could have gone to a priest for support and assistance. No matter what issue they present, I often find they're really looking for spiritual direction and insight—not something I'm equipped to provide—and they become frustrated.

In my practice I've met gay men who called themselves "recovering Catholics." They spent years in therapy, trying to undo the damage of hearing, throughout their lives, that gay sex is an "abomination" and that they'll go to hell if they "practice" it.

In my groups, I always tell the men, "A new member will be starting next week." That's typically all I say about someone new. Father Arturo, as I'll call him, entered the group, admitted he was sexually active, and said he needed to talk about being gay—then identified himself as a priest. The group (85 percent Catholic) had a very negative reaction. One member told me I should have "warned" them that Father Arturo was coming so they could prepare themselves or leave before he arrived. I wasn't aware of the strong judgment that many gay Catholic men hold against priests, and I simply wasn't prepared for how they would respond to a sexually active one.

While growing up, these men felt wounded by priests. Father Arturo was the lightning rod for all of their anger and sorrow. But he was up for the challenge. He raised all sorts of new issues— which everyone could work on and explore more fully. It became a therapeutic opportunity, not just for the group, but for Father Arturo. Through these other men's judgments, he was forced to work through his own issues about being gay and sexually active.

I joke that I'm glad to be Jewish, because much of what I learned in Hebrew school was conducted primarily in Hebrew. Even if the rabbi had spoken against homosexuality as a sin and an abomination, I wouldn't have understood a word he said. This always gets a laugh.

As we know, children are taught not to act, feel, or think in certain ways, and not to experience all their bodily sensations. At various workshops I've conducted, gay men have itemized the various "don'ts" they received as boys:

* "Don't act like a sissy."
* "Don't be a crybaby."
* "Don't touch yourself down there."
* "Don't aspire to be a ballet dancer, artist, musician, or actor."
* "Don't sit with your legs crossed."
* "Don't shake hands like a limp fish."
* "Don't look at or touch other boys and don't let them touch you."

These admonitions are all inherently sexist. If there's anything "feminine" about a boy, our social conventions lead us to believe there must be something wrong with him. Implicit in these elements of our culture is the message that there's something wrong with females. Yet we don't restrict girls in the same way. It's fine for them to play sports or to wear a suit and a tie to work. Girls are allowed to touch each other's hair and bodies, hug each other, and even go to the bathroom together.

I think this is why young gay men become aware of their orientation earlier than lesbians do. When we want to touch other boys, when we want to play with "girl things," we quickly realize we're different. Not until later do girls discover it's "wrong" to enjoy physical intimacy with each other.

One of my clients was told, "Men shouldn't be vulnerable." Another was warned, "Don't let others know your business." Boys who accept these messages find it hard to let others into their lives and to be open about their "vulnerability." This problem isn't specific to gay men; everyone has to grapple with repressive social messages.

How Gay Boys Are Wounded

Erik Erikson described the stages of physical, emotional, and psychological development from childhood into adulthood. He assigned specific developmental issues or "tasks," as he called them, to each psychosocial stage. He believed that if any stage was vandalized or interrupted, the child would suffer throughout his adult life until he resolved his wounding from that stage. *The Life Cycle Completed*[1] explains in detail each of these psychological stages. I'll cover just the ones most pertinent to gay men.

The Play-age Child or, as we would call him today, the preschooler (age 2-6), begins to initiate games and pretend stories, not just imitate others on the playground. At this stage, he develops a sense of right and wrong and starts to develop a sense of purpose and identity by dressing up in adult clothes, playing with dolls and action figures, trucks and cranes, and other goal-oriented toys.

At this stage, a gay boy suffers early wounding and other negative influences. As soon as he starts to display an affinity for feminine toys, his father often distances himself from his "sissy" son. The father might even be critical and shaming. In *The "Sissy Boy Syndrome" and the Development of Homosexuality*, Richard Green reports a study in which 75 percent of boys who played with female toys and identified with girls grew up to be gay.[2] Girl-play doesn't *make* a boy gay, but it's one of the early indicators that he is. (Also, let me note in passing that not all gay boys play with girls' toys, and bisexual and transgender children offer a variety of early indicators of their individual identities.)

We expect a good father to interact with his children, but because boys aren't supposed to play with dolls, they are rarely allowed time to "practice" this adult role-playing as children. When my first nephew was born, and my sister let me hold him or change his diaper, I had no idea what I was doing. Having never been allowed to play with dolls, I was never conditioned to know what to do.

I can't tell you how many LGBTQ individuals—at my workshops, in group therapy, and in individual therapy in my office—have cried over memories of being told that wanting to play like the opposite gender was wrong. Obviously, this kind of shaming can have effects that last into adulthood.

If a young gay boy's caregivers encourage him at this stage, then he'll feel free to use his imagination and engage in make-believe and role-playing without having to hide, without feeling shame or guilt about what comes naturally to him.

During a boy's *School-age* years, (approximately 6-12), he must develop competence and a sense of achievement by completing tasks and following directions. He develops a sense of self-worth. Here, caregivers and teachers must afford children intellectual stimulation and help them to acquire skills that will enable them to be productive and successful. If children don't develop a sense of competence, they instead form a sense of inferiority. As adults, they can become obsessively competitive with others. In my practice—and in the gay community in general—I see lots of insecure people with strong tendencies to compete. They have to "keep up with the Joneses" to feel good about themselves. Many of them feel threatened by other gay men's successes, relationships, and social and monetary status.

This particular neurosis is a conditioned trait in American culture, but for gay men it's more than that. Most gay boys get grief because they throw a ball like a girl, sit like a girl, can't fight, and don't fit in groups with other boys because they're different. They begin to feel totally incompetent as men. This is a huge issue that we explore in workshops. Our masculinity has been wounded as a result of the many negative messages we've received.

For the most part, heterosexual men find sports to be a good outlet for healthy (and sometimes unhealthy) competition. But we gay men tend to go to a gym rather than join a team. As a result, there's a lot of unhealthy competing over looks, muscles, and endowment.

Perhaps our worst wounds occur during *Adolescence*, between ages 12 and 18. Here all the earlier stages become integrated. Does the young man display a strong sense of independence, a basic sense of trust, and strong feelings of competence? Does he feel in control of his life? According to Erikson, adolescence is the most crucial stage. If the individual can manage this crisis successfully by integrating all the stages in a healthy way, he'll be ready to head out into the world and plan for his future. If not, however, the teen will feel incompetent, have difficulty making decisions, and remain confused about his sexual orientation, future career, and his role in life in general. In addition to the normal pitfalls that Erikson talks about, LGBTQ adolescents face additional challenges. These teens are confused about their sexual identity largely because they're not allowed to explore it in a healthy, productive way.

During this period of "identity crisis," a teen develops his authentic self. To figure out who he really is, he hangs out with peer groups who give him a sense of belonging. He tries to assemble a coherent self-image from an array of many different roles: jock, leather-jacketed rebel, SAT scholar, computer geek, "most popular" or "most likely to succeed," or just all-around good guy. At school, he'll develop a stronger sense of self, become separate from—which isn't to say rebellious against—his parents, and feel a sense of belonging.

A gay teenager is robbed of his sense of belonging. He has to play at heterosexuality, date girls, and pretend to be someone he's not. The negative impact is profound.

The Importance of Learning How to Be Intimate

Erickson refers to the next developmental stage as the *Young Adult* years (ages 19-40). Here the choice is between personal commitment to another human being (in the role of partner, spouse, or parent) and isolation. The young man learns about sex, love, and intimacy. His task is to integrate sex with romance and infatuation.

Erikson believed that no matter how successful a man is, he's not developmentally complete without *intimacy*. If all goes well, the young adult bonds with others and enjoys a secure sense of identity. If not, he'll fear commitment and find it difficult to depend on anyone.

Many gay men find themselves isolated because homophobia and heterosexism have kept them from developing intimacy skills.

Unfortunately, in young adulthood, gay males often feel forced to role-play heterosexuality. In an episode of the sitcom

Will and Grace, Will's acting teacher asks whether Will has any acting experience. He tells her that he acted as a straight man for about 19 years. She responds, "Not very well, I imagine!" Funny as that may be, it's sad that a young man should have to pretend to be anything other than who he really is.

In his book *Now That I'm Out, What Do I Do?* Brian McNaught writes that most gay men "have been enormously, if not consciously, traumatized by the social pressure they felt to identify and behave as... heterosexual, even though such pressure is not classified as sexual abuse by experts in the field. Imagine how today's society would respond if heterosexual 13-to-19-year-olds were forced to date someone of the same sex. What would the reaction be if they were expected to hold the hand of, slow dance with, hug, kiss and say, 'I love you' to someone to whom they were not... sexually attracted? The public would be outraged. Adult supervisors would be sent to prison. Youthful "perpetrators" would be expelled from school. Years of therapy would be prescribed for the innocent victims of such abuse... Yet, that's part of everyday life of gay teenagers."[3]

Psychotherapy Can Help

The type of therapy I offer gay men is similar, in many ways, to what I provide for clients who were sexually abused in childhood. Typically, gay men have suffered the kind of covert *cultural* sexual abuse noted above, and therapy needs to address that particular experience.

Some therapists simply present themselves as a blank screen, showing little or no emotion ("flat affect," the term is) and providing minimum feedback. They do not share anything about themselves with the client. In effect, they hope to hold up a mirror for their clients to offer them an opportunity to examine their own projections. This type of therapy has its place, but because the typical gay man entering therapy has a long history of emotional (and romantic) disconnections, this approach usually isn't effective.

For a sexual abuse survivor, the "blank screen" approach is ineffective for the same reasons. The world in which he lives is already a blank screen; the heterosexual culture's lack of response to a gay man's suffering is a primary cause of his psychological distress. His therapist's keeping him at an emotional arm's length only reinforces his original frustration when he found himself unable to connect to society at large. To heal a gay man who feels isolated and alone, safety and trust are essential within the therapeutic relationship. It's no help to him to have a therapist merely sit and nod and give no feedback.

Individual therapy can help heal the wounds a gay child sustains when his early attempts to learn attachment skills are frustrated. If his mother was overly protective (attached) and his father overly detached, the young gay child learns that love is either from a distance or overly close—"enmeshed," as psychologists call it. Thus, as an adult, he might either keep too much distance between himself and friends and partners or tend to get too close.

I try to help gay men learn that love is a balance of togetherness and separateness and that going too far in either direction isn't healthy. The therapeutic relationship serves as a model for that. We establish healthy boundaries while cultivating a feeling of closeness and healthy dependency.

In individual therapy, as we've learned, the client projects or transfers onto the therapist the traits of his early childhood caretakers. *Positive transference* happens when positive attributes are transferred onto the therapist. *Negative transference* occurs when negative attributes are transferred. This also happens with our coworkers and friends—and particularly our partners, as you'll see in Chapter 9. The more emotionally close you are to someone, the more the transference will emerge.

In therapy, however, we invite transference and talk about it. The client *should* transfer those negative feelings and images onto a therapist, which enables him to travel back in time to when he was a child and experience them again—only this time, with a different, better outcome. Now, with adult intelligence and maturity—and a therapist's help—the client is able to associate his feelings with a positive experience, thereby healing old wounds.

Positive and negative transference is especially important in dealing with gay issues. Clients who start work with me have a wide spectrum of feelings about my being an openly gay therapist. Some come wanting at least some of the life I enjoy: partnered, successful in business, and completely out. They enter therapy on a high because they believe I can help them get where they want to be. They idealize me, thus positively transferring onto me all the things they want. However, after a few sessions or even a few months, they begin to recognize that it took me years of effort to become comfortable with myself as a gay man. They hadn't anticipated the work involved.

And so the negative transference begins. Some clients become angry and say things like, "You can't help me" or "I can't have what you have." They either drop out of therapy or, if they continue, blame me for causing them "too much pain." In time, they realize that their own blocks are the only things standing in their way. It may be that they had a parent who neglected them and did not offer adequate guidance—or any guidance for that matter—particularly around being gay. As a client feels more dependent in therapy, the therapeutic relationship will resemble the dependent relationships of his childhood. I become a stand-in for that neglectful parent.

This is a natural, positive indicator that a client's psychological work has begun. He begins to appreciate the struggle involved in becoming a self-actualized, self-affirming gay man. If he steps up to this challenge, he enters his own therapy.

As you'll see in Chapters 9 and 10, negative transference is a major stumbling block for gay men in intimate adult relationships, because as boys and young adults, few of us enjoyed positive, non-sexualized interactions with other gay men. If clients can understand that their current feelings are reflections of their childhood experiences—which are not "ancient history" but rather drivers of their current problems—then they can work with me to get past the past and be primed for healthy adult love relationships.

For a gay man, entering a therapeutic relationship with an openly gay therapist is often very challenging. It may be the first time he's looked at himself and another gay man in an authentic way or talked to another gay male outside of a dark bar with loud music and alcohol. Ironically, another gay man's inviting him into a healthy space for the first time can be very frightening, because the relationship demands a level of intimacy, honesty, and authenticity he has never encountered. Just uttering the words "I might be gay" to another gay man produces anxiety.

An internal fight begins. He's violating the taboo that all men—gay, bisexual, and straight alike—have been taught: It's not okay to talk to another man openly except with scorn and contempt. When this taboo emerges, my client will often feel the need to run away from me. But for anyone just coming out, this experience can also be very exciting, too. For the first time he can openly and intimately explore his own orientation safely.

Anyone who's been out for a while and involved in the gay community has already formed ideas of what it is to be gay. If I challenge his thinking or offer him new insights, he may argue that I'm pushing an idea that doesn't jibe with his experience. My job isn't to tell a client who to be, but simply to share with him the things I perceive. Even a gay man who's been out for a while may not see his own subtle forms of internalized homophobia.

John Is "Out" But Not Really

John had been out for more than 20 years, but in my work with him, I soon discovered he had a limited awareness of most aspects of gay life. For the past decade, being out for John had meant going to the bars and being on gay apps, so this was all he knew. Now that he was in his 40s, he felt that gay men were rejecting him, which he attributed to the gay culture's premium on youth. As we know, men in general can be that way, and—yes—a lot of gay men seek only younger men. However, countless gay men have interests that aren't so narrow. They don't tend to hang out in bars, and John simply hadn't met them.

He didn't believe me when I told him the gay world was bigger than he imagined, but he did continue with therapy. Through our work together, he gathered the courage to attend Gay Pride events, where he found men who were interested in him. He happily admitted that he needed to expand his notions of what gay life was all about.

Therapy offers a safe place for a client to increase his self-awareness. As transference develops, it's normal for him to bypass (consciously or not) the work he thought he came into therapy to do. Little does he know this shift in priorities *is* his work. The client will say to me, "You're comfortable with being gay only because you have a relationship" or "Yeah, if I were successful like you, I could afford to be out and open too." What he doesn't know is that before I met Mike and my career took off, I was just as out and open as I am now. But again, this resistance is a positive indication that a client has begun his therapy. Those are *his* judgments and *his* projections—windows into who he is, clues that help me get to know him better and help him get to know himself.

I'm the Man Your Parents Warned You About

Sometimes my being gay elicits intense homophobia from a client. I become a container for all his rage and frustration. Some therapists are so uncomfortable with the anger that arises from negative transference that they won't explore these projections. Either they find they can't help the client or they find other, less confrontational, ways to do so. But I strongly believe in letting these feelings emerge. I'm the lightning rod for the client, a stand-in for whomever he *really* needs to be angry with. The negative transference is coded information about him.

The purpose of decoding negative transference isn't to find someone to blame. It's about identifying who the anger really is directed at. The client can direct it toward me first, and then we can figure out together who it really belongs to. Sometimes clients want to confront the actual perpetrators to "clear the air," but it's safer—and usually more effective—to bring out what's been suppressed within the safe space of therapy and to work it out there. If a client needs to go to the people who originally hurt him later, that's a choice I often support. It can be helpful, but not before doing the therapy work first.

I often refer to the "old mental tapes" that we all carry with us. They begin to play as soon as we encounter difficult situations. If our current situation aligns with what we were taught, then our tapes "match up" with reality and cause no problems. But if reality contradicts what we were taught, the tapes cause conflict. Obviously, changing our tapes is more helpful than trying to alter—or worse, deny—reality.

In therapy, of course, every known homophobic tape is activated. In a twist on the old joke, I become the very man your parents warned you about.

As a therapist, I believe I'm hired not only to be supportive and hold open an affectionate space for a client but also to be challenging and controversial. I don't fight with clients or cause any unnecessary pain, but I do point out occasions when something they say works against the inner and outer goals they've said they want to achieve.

In the next chapter, you'll see how partners seek "escape routes" when a relationship gets too intense and their partner gets too close. The same holds true in therapy. When a gay man starts feeling too close to me or we get too near an issue, I notice he'll react in one or more of the following ways:

1) Drop out of therapy.

2) Decide to see another therapist.

3) Rely on defenses like avoidance and resistance within therapy.

These exits are typical of many people in therapy, but with gay men, I see them more often. When clients resort to these exit strategies, I try to push them, gently and compassionately, to stay with and move through their pain. I'm like the guy who spots you in the gym to help you lift that heavier weight you're not yet strong enough to lift alone.

Gay clients often find it harder to "stick" with their pain. Moreover, a gay male therapist can make a client wonder, "Am I getting too close to this guy?" even if he knows that any good therapist has numerous boundaries in place. This is where issues of attachment, competence, and intimacy all surface for the client as well as for me. Revisiting even the happiest childhood can be a perilous journey, and some clients try to salve their own fear by drawing me out. They do this by trying to get into my personal life by asking me questions about myself and putting the focus on me. By not exposing the private aspects of my life, I keep the boundaries safe for the client. But being open about some aspects of my life can be very helpful. It can also help him decide my life is *not* the way he wants to live. What's important is that a client has some positive images of what gay life is all about.

Gay Homonegativity

Transference toward me is only one way in which clients express negative feelings about gay life. Many complain about effeminate gays and drag queens. This internalized homophobia can only damage their self-esteem and future attempts at friendships in the gay community.

In therapy, some clients speak contemptuously about "gay ghettos." They insist we shouldn't separate ourselves from our straight counterparts. I ask, "Do you have the same feelings about Jewish neighborhoods, Little Italy, or Chinatown, where other minorities have settled?" Their usual answer is, "Uh, no."

Jeff, 39, was the top executive at a high-powered advertising agency. Three years earlier, he'd divorced his wife of 15 years to live with a male partner. He came to me because he was troubled by his sexual behavior outside of his relationship.

In our first session, Jeff said, "I'm sure you and your partner aren't monogamous. Each of you must sleep around. That's just how gay life is. So how can you help me be monogamous and fit heterosexual standards onto my relationship?" Of course, Jeff was simply projecting.

He talked about going to a party where he turned around to see his partner French-kissing another guy. He said I'd understand, "because that must happen at parties that you attend." He insisted that I couldn't appreciate many aspects of his situation, because he'd been married to a woman and I hadn't. Another time, he began to weep because he felt I judged him for wanting to share a life with his partner that mirrored his notion of a heterosexual ideal.

Once I'd taught him about transference, both positive and negative, and the concept of projections, Jeff's therapy workout began in earnest, and he was able to find his own answers. We sorted through his various statements and used them as clues to help him discover who he was.

Right off, I told him that I *did* believe in monogamy. I told him I'd be horrified to see my husband French-kissing another man. That wasn't acceptable for us; it did *not* happen at any of the parties we attended. He thought I supported promiscuity because I was gay. That, I explained, was his own homophobic projection.

Truth is, gay men are divided on monogamy. We just talk more openly about it than straight couples. (See Chapter 5 and Chapter 10.) Yes, some segments of the gay culture accept open relationships, but others don't. I assured Jeff that he could find gay friends who were either monogamous or who at least respected his and his partner's boundaries.

I agreed with Jeff that I don't know all the nuances of heterosexual marriage. But I've treated hundreds of men who were married, and I was open to learning more. Jeff's fear that he couldn't be understood was another instance of transference. During his marriage, he believed that if he told people his real feelings, no one would understand. This problem went back to his childhood. When little Jeffrey tried to talk about a problem, his parents wouldn't give him any time or attention, and he felt misunderstood. Now he was projecting these old feelings onto me.

Jeff understood that much of what he saw in gay life reflected his own limited awareness about being gay. He was able to identify his negative transference toward me as his resentment toward his parents (as well as toward some gay men who'd harshly judged him for wanting to apply heterosexual standards to his relationship with his partner). He wanted to be conservative, monogamous, and have a stable circle of friends. To move in that direction, he went through lots of tears, anger, sadness, and joy.

It's okay to argue. Let differences exist. If my opinions don't work for a client, sometimes he'll say, "Joe, that's what works for you, but not for me." I accept that.

Therapy is about owning—and taking charge of—your own thoughts, judgments, feelings, transference, and projections. This means tracking them back to the source to examine what they tell you about yourself.

A heterosexual therapist offers gay men other types of beneficial transference challenges. The client may worry that his therapist will try to make him straight (as his parents may have done)—or even hope the therapist will try and succeed! The straight male therapist can also stand in for society as a whole or represent the heterosexual privileges that a gay man will lose by coming out. Working with a straight therapist who is willing to tackle these issues can be very rewarding and healing.

Group Therapy Affirms and Challenges

Group therapy offers gay men a sense of belonging and helps them develop social skills they never had a chance to practice in childhood. This can be a client's first experience of a group of other gay men in a setting with the lights on and no chemicals or sex involved. In the first group session I ran, every gay man was tense, anxious, and nervous, including myself. It was new terrain for all of us.

Whatever a man's doing out in the real world, for good or ill, he'll bring it with him into group therapy. Once he enters group, I see how he relates to others and how others relate to him—live, unplugged, and uncensored. I can intervene, interpret, and give feedback on the spot so that his future encounters can have healthier outcomes.

Your first group was the family that shaped you. Inevitably, someone in group therapy will remind you of your mother, father, brother, or sister. These similarities offer many opportunities to heal as you re-experience that familiar energy—this time, with the possibility of a different outcome.

Your second group was the one which helped you learn to socialize. Again, someone here will remind you of an old friend, boss, bully, neighbor, rabbi, priest, ex-partner or someone who was important in the years you ventured away from your family into the schools and religious institutions you attended. Again, opportunities arise for some healing work to be done with these "stand-ins" in the group.

Getting gay men to both enter and participate in a gay men's group is a challenge. The first thing I almost always hear is, "I don't want to sit in a room full of queens feeling like victims and bitching about their lives." I reply that the group isn't like that at all—griping and whining aren't allowed. Either men do their work or they leave.

Some say they want feedback from a professional like me but not from other "screwed-up" people like themselves. I point out that these group members are their peers, not authority figures. All too often, individual therapy is a one-sided relationship where the client speaks only about himself and there's a limit to what I can contribute in terms of my own personal insights and struggles. (A therapist has to keep a certain impersonal distance so that the therapeutic experience stays therapeutic.) In a gay men's group, each man shares his personal struggles and hears (and reacts to) the judgments of the other guys in the group. What's important is the peer-to-peer sharing. I'm on hand to step in if someone offers inappropriate or unhelpful feedback.

Which isn't to say group sessions aren't sometimes rough-and-tumble. You will want to hear even misguided judgments and reactions, because these challenges to your self-representation will prepare you for what you regularly encounter "out there" in real life.

Transference and projection arise in group just as in individual therapy. As I mentioned earlier, one member may remind another of a relative or past partner. Another man may have a bad reaction to another group member, or even develop romantic feelings for him. This lively interaction provides a rich opportunity for insight, growth, and healing. This is why a combination of group and individual therapy is ideal. Gay clients can work out their intimacy issues privately, then bring what they've learned to their group.

Whenever a member voices frustration about how the group is operating, others usually join in. This is typical behavior as the men learn how to empower themselves. In a gay men's group with a gay therapist, however, I've found the "complaint chorus" is more forceful and bullying than in a mixed gay-straight group. But this important acting-out allows more family dynamics to arise. How were you treated while growing up within your family? What's it like to have the support of other group members (your siblings) lobbying against Dad (the therapist)? How were you treated as a gay male? Exploring these issues can help heal childhood wounds.

Group Guidelines for Safety

To ensure emotional and physical safety, I enforce a few non-negotiable guidelines. The most important of these is confidentiality. Any gay community is small enough that group members might have friends in common. Therefore, respecting every man's confidences is imperative, during group and in all the years following, so that no one needs to worry about being "outed" as having attended group therapy.

No group member is allowed to be sexual, date, or even socialize with any other member. There are strong reasons for this. First, the group is where *all* the work needs to be done. Problems can arise if outside subgroups or friendships develop. One man may innocently tell another something he doesn't want mentioned in front of the others. This erodes the principle that all admissions must stay within the confines of the group. Having to keep secrets drove men to enter group therapy in the first place, and private "sharings" tend to dilute the group's energy and overall purpose.

Only the chemical-free may attend. If a participant is taking prescribed medications, fine. But if he's had even one drink for dinner, I ask him to leave. One group member confided that he was high on marijuana. He argued that if he stated the truth, he deserved to stay. He wasn't willing to look at his drug-use problem, so he blamed me and the group when I asked him to leave. (This is a good example of negative transference.) He had broken the agreed-upon group contract of not using nonprescribed drugs, and he was not willing to take responsibility for that.

The group triggers feelings and runs on emotions; anyone who suppresses them with nonprescribed drugs or alcohol is hindering our collective effort. Therapy can't work if someone's mood and mind are altered. Moreover, some members are in recovery from alcohol or drugs. It just makes sense to keep group sessions drug-free.

Group is all about forging and exploring relationships with other gay men. You'll get support from others, but you must be there for them as well. Given our strong hardwiring *not* to be there for other gay men, this is sometimes difficult. When you're single, it's so much easier. You can pick and choose the experiences you want, deciding exactly how much—or how little—energy you want to devote to them. This is also true for individual therapy. It's up to you how much you want to share, at your own pace. But in group, just as with a partner, the need for cooperation figures in the equation. We meet each week. No matter what your expectations, you have to be there on time and ready to go wherever the process takes us all.

For a few weeks, you can choose not to share anything personal. Just sitting and listening to others' work will trigger your own thoughts and feelings. You'll be doing work on your own, whether you know it or not.

You'll learn insights and techniques you'll need in any relationship with a partner. You can seldom predict what someone else will say, or what feelings and thoughts will arise. Similarly, in relationships, you don't know what your day-to-day interactions with your partner will generate. To achieve intimacy, living with— and learning from—uncertainty is a must. Any relationship pulls you into uncharted terrain, whether or not you want to go there. And that's a good thing!

Will and Mario

In one group session, Will discussed his guilt about coming out to some of his family but not others. Mario, another group member, turned to him and said, "I'm tired of hearing that story over and over again. You need to move on."

Will was very upset: "This is supposed to be a safe place for me to talk about my feelings without judgment!"

Mario insisted that he'd meant it in a kind, loving way. He felt that Will was stuck and needed to hear that kind of feedback, and Mario *was* tired of hearing the story.

Will became very angry and threatened to leave the group. Mario began to cry and stated that he, too, thought this was a place where, "I could express myself and not have to hold back."

Yes, the group is a safe place to let your feelings, thoughts, and story unfold. But safety doesn't mean no one will ever challenge you. It does mean no one will call you hurtful names, abandon you emotionally or physically, or disrespect your most heartfelt feelings. You deserve respect, and the other group members deserve respect from you.

Mario had every right to give Will feedback, though the group process demanded that Mario examine his feelings, too. Other group members didn't have the same reaction. So, as any group should, we helped Mario explore what in *his* history had made him especially sensitive to Will's repeating his story.

We discovered that while Mario was growing up, his parents recycled their own hassles over and over, without ever working through the issues or trying to heal them. Their endless repetition of gripes made Mario frustrated and confused. Mario began to see that Will's case was different—he *needed* to recycle his story for a while to make progress and work through his guilt. Once Mario recognized where his frustration with Will was coming from, he started to move toward working on the issue with his parents. Will turned out to be the catalyst for this work.

Then, of course, we had to look at why Will was angry with Mario. True, many people would be have been angered by Mario's comment, but Will's loud reaction and desire to leave indicated something deeper than a simple reaction to Mario.

After Will calmed down, he said he'd "heard" Mario tell him his work was wrong and that he was getting nowhere. This, of course, was the same message his own family still sent him. Whenever Will made progress, his family simply downplayed it, which made him feel "bad" and "wrong." Quite unsuspectingly, Mario had stepped into Will's long-standing resentment. Will had "heard" Mario echo the tape Will ran in his own head.

Mario was honestly interested in Will's progress, and his wanting Will to move on did come from his concern that Will not stay stuck. Indeed, in Will's family, staying stuck was actually rewarded. No one had ever challenged him to do better. So instead of seeing the care—something foreign to Will—behind Mario's remark, he felt only the hurt that accompanied his belief that he'd made yet another "bad decision."

Group Therapy Is a Unique Opportunity to Heal

In individual therapy, insights like Will's do occur from time to time between therapist and client. In group, however, there's a much greater likelihood that such insights will happen, and happen much faster, because everyone is self-disclosing. All the members of the group learn from all exchanges, which helps to deepen their work. Mario and Will wouldn't have perceived the issues underlying their reactions without the help of the other group members and me.

Obviously group can be very intense. Like Will and Mario, members never know what will trigger a confrontation. Again, a confrontation is a positive indicator that the group is on the right track, but it can make meetings scary to attend.

Group is about intimacy—learning what it's like to be close to other gay men. Week by week, the men get emotionally more familiar with one another. It's hard not to, when they're disclosing vital, personal aspects of their lives. This is the reason for the rule that anyone planning to leave must give the group at least three weeks' notice. Most people have a hard time saying goodbye. If you've been a group member for months or years, and then you call me to say, "I'm done with group. I'm not coming back," or, worse, simply disappear without a word to anyone, then you dishonor the men who've shared your confidences.

On the first week of his termination, a man announces that he's leaving and explains his decision. The next week, he says goodbye to each group member and talks about how each man touched him and describes what he's taking from his experience with them all. On the last week, each man, including me, says goodbye. Other members give him feedback to let him know what they hope he'll continue to work on.

As you'll see in Chapters 9 and 10, romantic long-term relationships bring on the unexpected. If you want things to go one way, the man in your life might have other ideas. Practicing these skills—not 24/7, but only once a week—is the luxury of group.

Group helps to heal gay men's deep hurt over not being witnessed. In a perfect world, you could say how you felt to someone who was bothering you—or whom you admired and liked—and he'd hear you. But even in the gay community, others often don't want to hear our personal stories or to help us examine our lives. Group demands that others listen to your pains and joys and that you witness theirs in return.

In most books, movies, and TV shows, romances are heterosexual. To relate to these stories, we gay men must identify with the woman or imagine the "hero" as gay. Either way, we're not given valid role models.

I recall the first time I watched a movie about gay men. Seeing two men having a deep relationship, kissing in a romantic way, or even flirting with one another brought tears to my eyes. The gay community desperately needs more positive, affirming images. Group brings similar "success stories" to life, and there's no need to "translate" heterosexual experiences into a gay context. Group members hear stories about gay men in the company of other men. Group members can picture themselves in these stories, and this therapeutic mirroring offers deep healing.

Missing a session may indicate a number of things. A member may rationalize that he's just giving himself a breather that night, but he could be missing a very important opportunity. Moreover, he sends the message that other group members aren't as important as he is, and that he doesn't feel an obligation to be there for them. As a result, I don't allow more than four absences a year. If a man cannot commit to this, he simply can't enter the group.

Commitment is a major issue for men in general and for gay men in particular. Individual therapy can be paced differently, so that the client can miss a few sessions or take breaks, but group invites a deeper level of commitment. You're creating new pathways for intimacy that will benefit you outside that group.

In a physical workout, you strain to lift weights so that when you leave the gym, you're stronger, fitter, and more self-confident. Individual therapy is like having a personal trainer. But as any body-builder will tell you, working out where other men are also sweating and struggling is a powerful inducement to complete your full regimen. (Couples, of course, already constitute their own "group," as you'll see in Chapters 9 and 10.)

Weekend Workshops Get Your Feet Wet

Many gay men avoid coming into therapy—like many straight people—because of the implication that if they have to do therapy, then they're weak and can't help themselves. This is partly why I do talks and hold weekend workshops. They let wary individuals attend something that doesn't have the "therapy" stigma. They meet me and see that I'm not so scary. They can get their feet wet with therapy without having to call it therapy.

Also, while workshops are not therapy, they are *therapeutic* and can become part of the healing for someone already in therapy. Attending workshops can speed up their process and offer insights that neither individual nor group therapy can offer. Just as group accelerates and deepens one's work in individual therapy, weekend workshops enhance the group therapy experience.

Partners who are afraid to enter therapy together can attend a "Getting The Love You Want" (GTLYW) couples workshop, become familiar with me and the material, and see for themselves whether they might want to venture into regular therapy. For gay men in ongoing individual or group therapy, attending a GTLYW couples workshop with their partner can be extremely beneficial. I used to work with individuals for long periods and spent a lot of time helping them heal and grow. But when they went back to their partners who weren't in the therapy loop, things between them would break down. My clients had learned a new way of living that was foreign to their partners, which tended to cause some turbulence or even jeopardize their relationships.

In the GTLYW workshop, couples are there together in the same room, which can be awkward at first, but by the middle of the workshop, couples begin to feel the advantages of each other's presence and interaction. There is no forced interaction between the couples, so that provides a level of comfort as well.

I encourage individuals I work with to participate in workshops with their partners. This is a way to bring their partners up to speed and teach them tools to keep communication lines open. Then, even though only one of them is in therapy, they both can grow together to ensure that their relationship stays whole and strong.

When Should You Seek Therapy?

So now you know the ins and outs of traditional psychotherapy. It can be a very productive place for you to do the kind of work you need to do to deal with your unresolved internalized homophobia from childhood, along with any family-of-origin work that you need to address. It can also become a place to deal with relationships; most importantly, your relationship with yourself.

When should you seek therapy? The "last straw" differs from person to person. You'll know it when it happens. Some destructive pattern in your life has just come up too many times, and you want things to be different. Nobody can decide for you what your last straw is, but when it happens, take the hint. Find a therapist. Join a group. Go to a workshop. Get help!

References

1. Erik H. Erikson and Joan M. Erikson. *The Life Cycle Completed* extended version. New York: W. W. Norton & Company, 1998.
2. Richard Green. *The "Sissy Boy Syndrome" and the Development of Homosexuality*. New Haven: Yale University Press, 1987.
3. Brian McNaught. *Now That I'm Out, What Do I Do?* New York: St. Martin's Press, 1997.

Chapter 8

Maintain Rewarding Relationships

You must be in gay community, before you can find gay friends and partners.

—Alexander Payne

Most gay men want friends. Many gay men want to date. But some gay men do not understand that they need to seek gay community. You especially need to put yourself in a gay context if you want to find friends and partners, but in general you need gay community to avoid the confusion and depression that goes with being socially isolated. When you have gay friends and acquaintances, you can join them for coffee, talk about past relationships and current problems, and receive the kind of mirroring and consolation that no straight acquaintance or relative could possible offer.

Isolation

Steve, 41 years old, had been out for a long while and had tended bar at a gay club before becoming an ad salesman. He came to me after his partner of five years said, "I'm leaving you."

Steve admitted that, overall, he had a negative view of gay culture. At the bar where he used to work he'd seen countless men date each other, only to break up in record time. Relationships seemed to last two months, tops.

During his 15 years as a bartender he'd struggled to find his own Mr. Right. But eventually he came to believe it simply wasn't possible. He assumed that gay culture was mostly accessible through the bar scene and gay apps, and he never considered exploring any other avenues.

Steve's eyes were warm and sensitive, which made his craggy features even more attractive. When he talked about his childhood, I saw that his parents had neglected him. They even nicknamed him Ugly—in an "endearing way," Steve said. Indeed, Steve *felt* ugly, which he attributed to a broken nose he'd suffered in a fistfight and to his aging body. In truth, Steve was a ruggedly handsome guy. His distinctive nose added to the attractive ruggedness he embodied. Just over 6 feet tall and well built, he had a pleasingly deep, resonant voice.

In high school, students had made fun of his nose. Girls didn't want to date him and called him "Bent-Nose." He described himself as heavy-set and awkward. But after he'd grown into his 20s, lost weight, and had an operation to straighten his nose a bit, men in gay bars pursued him. According to Steve, the bar hired him because he was "good-looking."

Still, Steve couldn't see himself this way, so his self-esteem depended on external compliments. After becoming an ad salesman, he met Todd at the bar where he used to work, though he never thought anything would come of the encounter. Todd was persistent in his pursuit of Steve. Soon they fell in love and moved in together. But during their years together as a couple, they had no gay friends in common.

Moreover, most of Steve's and Todd's friends were straight women. Now that Todd had asked for a divorce, Steve found companionship with women whom he loved dearly, and who loved him in return. But he wasn't connected to any other gay men, even as acquaintances.

His coming to see me was a big step, since he didn't trust gay men very much – his only encounters had been in bars, and in the gyms where he'd worked out. Steve told me that gay culture was just based on sex. He believed he'd never find another partner because he saw his meeting Todd as a fluke, a once-in-a-lifetime event that now was ending.

He'd tried everything he could to convince Todd to stay, but to no avail. Todd was frustrated. He couldn't induce Steve to buy a house or go out more in the gay community. So, after long consideration, Todd decided to end their relationship. He felt—wrongly!—that their inevitable power struggle (which I'll explain fully in Chapter 9) indicated that their connection was hopeless.

Now Steve was alone, with no gay friends, feeling empty and isolated. I invited him to enter my gay men's therapy group. Due to constraints on his time and finances, he didn't want to make the weekly commitment. I also encouraged him to attend my gay men's workshop, which was less costly and time-consuming and offered an opportunity for contacts with other gay men.

Steve declined. His goals in therapy were to work through his grief over the loss of Todd and to adjust to a single life without any gay friends. He did start to date through various apps, but these encounters only confirmed his belief that he had no hope of finding lasting love as a gay man.

As he began to feel less depressed, he came to his appointments less frequently. Finally, he admitted that money was the issue now that his partner had moved out and he was paying the rent by himself. He soon terminated therapy.

Steve's resistance to new friendships with gay men caused him a lot of problems. It contributed to an even longer period of grieving over the loss of his partner and only worsened his isolation. Many clients use lack of time and money as excuses to abandon their therapy. But I've noticed that people usually make time—and find the money—to do the things they really want to do. Steve resisted going to the emotional places he needed to. I suspect that from the start he'd never found a secure place for himself within his family. Because of his parents' neglect and emotional abuse, it seemed "normal" to Steve when his schoolmates treated him with the same disrespect.

On a conscious or unconscious level, peer perpetrators—of any age—often know whom they can pick on. Their victim might as well be wearing a neon sign on his forehead, but he doesn't know he's wearing it. If the child—or adult—never fights back, his predicament only gets worse.

Steve never fought back; he just took the abuse, which further damaged his self-esteem. Now, as an adult, he perpetuated the conditions of his isolation. He was extremely reluctant to socialize with others—particularly with gay men, who reminded him of the pain of Todd's rejection and the cruelty of his peers in his schooldays.

Breaking up is different for gay men. Straight men usually get sympathy from family and friends, who try to "fix up" the lonely guy. This generally doesn't happen for us, because our straight friends and family members usually don't know other gay men to fix us up with. Nor are they always eager to see us partnered. A single gay man is less conspicuous, so his family may be secretly relieved not to have to deal with his partner. If he is connected to the gay community, a gay man can find other gay men to talk to. He can receive a sympathy and understanding difficult to find in the straight world.

By not allowing himself to maintain gay friends during his relationship, Steve had left himself vulnerable. Bars and gyms—where shallow encounters and the expectation of speedy gratification are the norm—don't give an accurate picture of what all of gay life is like.

Steve resisted gay men's group therapy, weekend workshops, and support groups because, unconsciously, he understood that participating in these activities would reawaken his feelings from childhood, when he didn't get acceptance from peers or family. The more I talked to him about this, the less often he came to therapy. He simply wasn't ready.

You Need Gay Community

Many gay men who come to my office play down their need to be in gay environments. They often talk about their desire to "blend in" and live a "mainstream" life where being gay isn't their primary identity. This is their personal choice, of course, but often these same men have difficulty finding gay friends and partners. Sadly, their internalized homophobia puts them in a bind: You can't expect to meet gay men if you never go to places where they're out and visible.

We have a parallel version of this syndrome within our own culture—straight women who choose to hang out primarily with gay men and their own girlfriends. They complain of not dating much, about not having boyfriends, and of their grief at being alone. I've always considered "fag hag" a brutal term, yet it's the label these women often give to themselves.

Like gay men who distance themselves from the gay community, these women cultivate habits that are isolating and self-defeating. But there are deeper issues here—for both the straight women and the gay men they hang with. Up front are fears of intimacy and self-esteem. A woman who's attracted to men but also fears them may pal around with "safe" hunks who won't hit on her. It's a no-risk relationship, with all sexual tension drained out.

Meanwhile, because their gay friends are clearly out of reach, isolated gay men feel safe. And for any gay man with internalized homophobia, a fag hag is a crutch for his self-esteem: Having a straight woman spend time with him makes him feel better about himself and improves his image in society. He can avoid homophobia by hiding behind her, and receive heterosexual privileges from others who think he is straight.

No religious family would move to a neighborhood where the nearest church or synagogue was 100 miles away, then complain about their isolation from others of their faith. This is the rationale for the "gay ghetto," where some men take comfort in the high proportion of other gay men. The goal isn't to limit their social spectrum but to end their isolation and increase the likelihood of meeting gay friends.

Another issue we have to face is our tendency to appropriate negative messages and judgments and to accept them as truths. In

"Multiple Mirroring with Lesbian and Gay Couples," a chapter in *Healing in the Relational Paradigm*, Sharon Kleinberg and Patricia Zorn explain how internalized homophobia manifests itself in gay and lesbian couples.[1] They begin by debunking the widely held myth that gay couples cannot survive. During "the power struggle," many gay couples assume this myth must be true. But all couples—gay and straight alike—go through this stage (see Chapter 9).

Zorn and Kleinberg address more subtle examples of internalized homophobia:

1. Trying to pass as straight even when it's safe to be out.

2. Not identifying yourself as gay even after you've been in a committed relationship for years.

3. Never announcing your anniversary to good straight friends because anniversaries aren't as "important" for gay couples.

4. Avoiding public displays of affection even where it's safe to do so.

5. Criticizing a partner for looking too effeminate.

As we observed earlier, many gay men have spent their entire lives avoiding each other as much as they can for fear of being discovered and scorned. In a bar with loud music and alcohol, the emotional distance between gay men could not be greater.

Other, better ways to meet men include activities at gay community centers; gay-friendly religious services; running, bicycling, bowling, and swimming clubs; Gay Pride parades and Pridefest; gay vacation packages through travel agents; and personal ads on the Internet. You can also volunteer for gay political and social groups or find employment at a gay or gay-friendly business.

If you can offer specialized services to these organizations, by all means do so. But don't forget, even a "menial" job like stuffing envelopes is an act of service that lets you begin to socialize with other gay men.

The Dating Jungle

Dating can be a barbaric experience, for straight, bisexual and gay folks alike. Participants don't know each other at the start and therefore lack any initial feelings of attachment. A number of my clients "hate" gay culture for being so visually oriented. I constantly remind them that this is a guy issue, not a gay issue. For better or worse, men generally seek partners who look good on the outside. Women do this, too, but from the earlier stages of dating, women tend to be attracted to more than just a handsome face or impressive body.

A client of mine proved this. He wrote a truthful personals ad, describing himself as "50 years old, overweight." He sent it to an online dating service to run under the "Men Looking for Men" heading.

By mistake, they placed his ad under "Men Looking for Women." He received responses from 15 ladies interested in dating him. He contacted the service and asked them to run his ad under the appropriate gay heading. When they did, he received not one response.

Women give men more leeway regarding physical appearance. Compared with their straight male counterparts, gay men are at a disadvantage. Prospective partners are less forgiving of a gay man's advancing age or protruding belly.

Many gay men come to my office anxious about their romantic prospects because they are not young and buff. Because they don't look like circuit boys, they belittle themselves and fear that their odds of linking up with another gay man are low to zilch.

I often find myself working as a dating coach as well as a psychotherapist. My clients deserve whatever I can give them. Look at your childhood, your adolescence, your past relationships. Do you keep finding men, over and over, with the same traits as the people who raised you? Or with the same traits as men you've been with before? If you don't resolve the issue, you will keep suffering your way through miserable relationships.

According to Imago Relationship theory (more about that in the next chapter), we find different "actors" to read from our old childhood scripts. As adults, we keep seeking—and finding!—understudies to read stale dialogue from our past family relationships. This is why people often find themselves in work situations that remind them of childhood experiences, or with "friends" who treat them in the same way relatives or schoolmates used to. Because this process is unconscious, it's imperative to make a *conscious* effort to stop recycling your past.

Clients who tell me, "I can't change it, so what's the point?" seldom realize they're rerunning yesterday's paradigms in the present.

Socially, we gay men can't always tell whether we're going out on a romantic date, or just as friends. I dated for ten years—and this uncertainty drove me crazy. Sometimes I'd find a guy very attractive and ask him out—only to discover, many weeks and many "dates" later, that while I was falling in love, he saw only a budding friendship.

It pays to remain close friends with men you've dated even after your romance has cooled. Yes, it can happen, with no resentment or jealousy. I once dated the rabbi who later conducted the ceremony at which Mike and I got married. Our best men were a couple, and I once dated one of them. Ironic, but it was such an honor to have these two be part of our ceremony. They had both helped me find the right partner.

One of our best men was Jeff. I'd dated him about eight times, though I never considered him my type. But, as with all of my other dating relationships, I approached him with an open mind.

At that time, I was adamant about not having sex until I felt comfortable. Jeff respected that. He was always courteous, and I began to really like him. He was stable, insightful, smart, and Jewish, like me.

I started to have feelings for him. Then, one night, he said he was getting back together with another man he'd dated before—he wanted to try to make their relationship work. He liked me, he said, but his heart was pulling him toward this other man (who, I'm delighted to say, has been his partner for more than 25 years). But back then, I was devastated. I'd taken a risk and found myself attached to this guy who decided to drop me.

We had a ritual: After each date, we walked around the large pond near his condominium. Right then, I just wanted to get in my car, race home, and cry my heart out. But instead, I stretched myself and walked around the water with him. We talked about what had been nice about dating each other. He kissed me goodbye, and I drove home—calm and sad.

Over the next few years, I grew to appreciate what Jeff had done. To my mind, he was a real *mensch*—strong, always honest with me, empathic, and respectful of what we'd had together during our eight dates. Now he's one of my best friends.

Yes, when someone says he's not interested in you, it hurts—but that's part of dating. Not every at-bat is a home run.

When I went out with Mike for the first time, he asked me, "Is this a date?" That was so nice, innocent, and brave that it grabbed my heart. How many men would have the nerve to ask that question and risk being told no?

Of course my answer was yes.

The second time, before Mike and I went out to dinner early in the evening, he asked me, "Are we still dating?" Another honest, direct, vulnerable question.

"My answer is yes—if you're still interested."

He was still interested. What if he hadn't been, or I hadn't? That's the unavoidable risk we all take. Most gay men have suffered in so many ways that they'll do anything to avoid rejection.

Even if you excel at what you do and get high praise from your bosses, coaches, and families, the prospect of rejection leaves your romantic heart at risk. But the alternatives—isolation and loneliness—are even scarier and more depressing.

Avoid Dating Pitfalls

I teach gay men to look at dating as a learning experience that teaches them how to turn negatives into positives. I know this isn't easy, but it's all about marketing oneself. The idea is to know the rules—and also to know when there really aren't any. Dating is about having fun while protecting your heart and ego. If you get rejected, it's not about your self-worth. As you recall from Chapter 1, judgments are 90 percent a reflection of the one doing the judging.

That may sound simplistic, but matters of the heart are never simple. I invite clients to venture into the dating arena with intentionality and consciousness. This strategy diminishes the chances of getting hurt—no matter the outcome—and allows you to learn more about yourself and the kind of men you want to meet.

Bypassing this leaves you stranded in emotional adolescence. During my own dating, I found that the men I chose—and who chose me—got better and better in terms of maturity, honesty, and integrity. Overall, I learned lots about myself. Who and what was right for me? Every okay guy I dated led me to a better guy. I learned from what I did—and didn't—enjoy about each person and experience. I became alert to those factors in my next relationship. I even formed friendships with some great men.

There are a few issues to approach cautiously. Don't let them become pitfalls for you.

First, clients often complain about the man who says he "wants a relationship" but his behavior doesn't bear this out. You go out with friends, and there he is at the bar, alone, looking to hook up. Or you see him on online apps. You confront him, and he denies that his behavior means anything. This doesn't mean he's "bad" or wrong, or even that he's lying to you. He may very well want a relationship, but he may not be ready for one. Also, he may not realize what it means to be in a relationship, or he may be unwilling to do the necessary work.

I encourage a client to talk to the other man about the lack of congruency between his words and his behavior— and about how my client feels about it. Then I tell him to stop torturing himself by listening only to the other guy's words. When words and actions don't fit together, it's time to move on.

Second, be wary of the man who just wants you for sex and nothing more. He may court you and flirt all night, saying you have nice eyes and a great personality. But afterward, you never see him again. Or if you do, he passes you by as if he's never seen you before. Obviously, this can be very hurtful—the more so if the experience was particularly pleasurable and you got your hopes up.

After encountering a number of men like this, I shifted from short-term, recreational dating to long-term, relationship-oriented dating. As I mentioned, I developed a cardinal rule—and boundaries—for myself: No sex before I was ready. Yes, this was difficult to bring off. Many an attractive man passed me by, but that was okay with me. If he couldn't wait and didn't feel connected or interested enough, then I decided he wasn't right for me. No shame or blame on either of us. In this way I avoided the hurt of having sex with the guy, only to have it turn out to be nothing.

When I share this with my clients, some look at me like I am crazy. "No sex! I could never do that!" I tell them, "You have to do what's right for you. *That's* what worked for me."

Third, and very important, when you're looking for a partner, how far along are each of you in your own coming-out process? Many openly gay clients, sadly, find boyfriends who are just barely out of the closet. Still, they crave a relationship. I've found that if one man is in the early stages of coming out, and his partner is further along, they're less likely to stay together.

Let's say that you're mostly out and living as a gay man in the fullest sense. You meet a guy who frets about what people might think about two men eating dinner together at a restaurant. Once he's your boyfriend, he never introduces you to his family. Even worse, he thinks it's weird for men to be romantic and playful outside the bedroom.

Beware! Differences in how *out* you both are can hinder the love you feel for each other.

Ted had been out of the closet his whole adult life. His relationship with Jonathan was his third and Jonathan's first. During their five years together, Ted wanted them to live together, but Jonathan resisted. He wasn't yet out to his family or his business partner. He didn't plan to come out anytime soon, and worried that living with Ted would be a red flag that he was gay.

This situation caused much friction when they got together on weekends. Whose apartment would they go to, given that one of them would have to pack a bag? Ted was frustrated; he contemplated breaking off the relationship even though he didn't want to. At Ted's insistence, he and Jonathan came to couples therapy with me.

Ultimately, Jonathan decided to talk to a younger cousin about his being gay and to bring Ted along to family functions. The cousin reacted negatively and told him never to bring up the subject again. Jonathan was devastated. Now he felt there was no way he could tell his immediate family—living with Ted was not an option. But Ted's parents welcomed Jonathan, and Ted resented not having the same opportunity with Jonathan's family.

They stayed in couples therapy for about three months, then cancelled their last appointment and stopped coming. Not long afterward, Jonathan called me, weeping, to say that Ted had just ended their relationship. Jonathan re-entered therapy with me, this time by himself. He and Ted had never lived together. Jonathan was still afraid to be seen with Ted, but now that their relationship was over, he tearfully stated that he'd do anything to save it, including coming out more. But it was too late. This time, Ted was serious—he was through with Jonathan.

Now, at age 39, Jonathan felt scared and alone. He was finally facing himself. I stressed the importance of coming out. Jonathan finally saw how his closetedness was ruining his life. Ironically, he was now finally willing to do the work toward coming out that he was unable to do within the relationship with Ted—though he bitterly lamented the cost he'd had to pay.

If you don't feel good about being gay—or your boyfriend doesn't—then one of you will keep his distance, and you'll never feel close. As you'll see in Chapter 9, differences can help strengthen a relationship, but this particular one can be toxic. This is especially true if the object of your affection, like Jonathan, isn't really interested in coming out at all.

Clients in the earlier stages of coming out complain of
volatile, short-term relationships, or of strong attractions to men
who are either straight or married. What better way to keep
emotional and physical distance?

Not that the partner who's more out can't assist the other to
come out more. That can strengthen the relationship. A man in
Stage One of coming out can fall in romantic love with another
guy whom he admires for being out even more. But I've seen
another problem there: As the more closeted man grows,
progressing through the later stages of coming out, he finds
himself no longer attracted to his boyfriend. He sees him in a
different, more realistic light. If their connection was based solely
on "outness," consciously or not, their relationship is in jeopardy.

Don, a 45-year-old lawyer, had been dating his boyfriend for
over a year. Up to that point, Don had been heterosexually married,
with no children, and was about to make partner in his firm. He'd
had very little time for himself and didn't come out until relatively
late in his life. While venturing out to a gay bar, he'd met 26-year-
old Martin, who was *very* much out of the closet. Don didn't like it
that Martin frequented the bars and drank a lot, but he was drawn
to Martin's relaxed, natural manner—and to how obviously
comfortable he was about being gay.

Don realized their age difference could be an issue, but he
rationalized that in "gay years," he too was around 25, at least
emotionally. With this frame of mind, he assumed they were a
good match.

Don spent most of his time with Martin and his bar friends,
who were wild and also drank heavily. One time, Martin verbally
abused Don in front of his friends and wouldn't stop, even at
Don's insistence. Martin would drive recklessly, with Don in the
passenger seat fearing for his life. Because he'd lent Martin
money, Don described himself to me as "a sugar daddy" and "a
cash cow."

I encouraged Don to enter my gay men's group therapy to
experience men who weren't just gay but dealing with other issues.

Don accepted and for two years, on a weekly basis, he began to examine his past.

Even as a child, Don was strongly drawn to art, in particular, painting. But Don's mother hid his interest from her husband, who was annoyed at his son's "artsy, effeminate" bent. When Don was a teenager, attending classes at a fine arts academy on weekends, his father was so embarrassed that he'd drop Don off four blocks away because he was afraid to be seen delivering his son to a "sissy" academy.

It was now obvious to Don why he had disowned the same aspects of himself that his father had disowned. At 45, he decided, "No more." But while coming out, he met Martin, who treated him much the same way his family had. (We all tend to replay familiar scripts simply *because* they're familiar—even if they flopped the first time around.)

Martin was unwilling to change his behavior. Still, Don was drawn to him. Yet as Don came out more and more, he found his relationship with Martin diminishing in importance. Ultimately, Don passed through all six stages of coming out and found the courage to break with Martin. He then met a man closer to his own age, both chronologically and emotionally, who had shared many of the same experiences. They developed a relationship, and Don left therapy. We agreed he was going in the right direction. May-December relationships can thrive only if both partners are willing to grow and to help each other pass through the emotional and coming-out stages.

The fourth pitfall to avoid in dating is about *nurturing*. Gay men sometimes get in trouble either by seeking a nurturing partner or by looking for someone who wants to be nurtured. As they said on *Seinfeld*, nothing wrong with that! But when Don said that he was Martin's "sugar daddy," he should have heard some warning bells in his own head. Many men and women—gay, bisexual, and straight—don't want to be accountable or responsible. They seek a partner or "long-term caretaker" to do it all for them.

The following questions may seem petty, but your answers can be symptomatic of problems to come:

1. Who pays for your meal?
2. Do you split the check?
3. Does he offer—ever?
4. Who phones or texts whom? Is it back and forth, or are you always leaving messages for him?
5. Who makes plans? Is it mutual?
6. Does he ask you questions and listen to your answers, or use them as a springboard to talk about himself?
7. Does he listen? If not, he's not ready to relate, reciprocate, and share.

Is Your Online Boyfriend a Catfish?
The fifth pitfall I find my clients falling into is the tricky business of managing relationships that begin online and seem to take forever (if ever) getting face-to-face.

A number of my gay clients use online services and gay apps to socialize. I think this can be a fine way to begin friendships and find potential partners, as well as to hook up for brief encounters. But I worry about two things: (1) People often represent themselves online different from how they really are. (This common situation now has its own term: "Catfishing.") (2) Some men socialize only online, and I believe it is all-round healthier to be able to meet and socialize face-to-face. I'm not saying never socialize online. I'm just saying be aware of catfishing and try to move your connections eventually into the physical world. Otherwise, you need to accept that these are fantasy connections that may reflect no physical reality at all.

Some men are shy and fearful in social situations. Their social anxiety deters them from joining organizations or going to bars. They feel very vulnerable and find it difficult to accept the rejection they feel when dating. So, instead they meet and socialize with people through social media.

I've had several clients who developed what they thought were very deep and loving connections without meeting the other for six months or a year or longer. They texted. They exchanged pictures. Finally, they met, and it was a catfish. The texts were lies; the pictures fakes.

The term "catfish" comes from a 2010 documentary film, *Catfish*, which tells the story of a guy fooled by a completely made-up online "lover." He'd received pictures, but they were of a professional model, and so on. The film was a critical and commercial success and led to an MTV reality show of the same name, where pretty much every anonymous "friend" turns out not to be who they represent themselves to be.

Despite these issues, I believe socializing online, even with the danger of catfishing, can have its place for a shy gay man and can be one of the stepping stones he uses to eventually develop a functional social life. He doesn't have to leave the house. He doesn't have to confront his crippling anxiety. For these men, online socializing is a way to start learning how to meet people and manage relationships.

Here's what I've noticed in several cases. A man will develop feelings of romantic love for his online contact. They'll text each other. They'll sext each other. My client will tell me, "I fell in love. The guy is telling me he's never loved anybody like me. He tells me his news before he tells anyone else." Even though this is a *pseudo*-relationship, I want to honor the fact that there's practice going on here. That is, it's a way to practice relationship skills. Just remember if you engage with a contact like this, much of it may not be real and you could be being catfished.

My client, Jordan, is a 40-year-old man who came to me for counseling several years ago. He was shy, filled with social anxiety, just coming out. He had cared for an aging parent for many years. The parent passed away, and then Jordan had to face the fact that he'd never really gone out into the gay community. He was especially inhibited by his fear of rejection because he was self-conscious about his looks. He feared he just wasn't young enough or handsome enough for anyone to want him.

Before he met me, he had signed up with the online dating site, Match.com, and he'd been successful in making some connections, all out-of-state, all without voice, cam, or Skype contact. One guy lived in Chicago, another in North Carolina. Jordan had almost daily email contact with these men.

When he came to see me, he knew these connections weren't all he wanted, but he didn't know what to do. I asked him, "Did you ever meet these people? Have you ever seen them on cams?" I explained about catfishing. I said to him, "I can't believe you would go on for over a year without taking a look at each other. It's 2015. Everyone's got a webcam. All you have to do is turn it on. Don't you think you should make sure these guys are for real?"

But he didn't want to do that. He didn't want to be seen himself. However, he showed me (supposedly) their pictures, and they looked very attractive. He showed me their texts, which were very intimate and affectionate. They said things like, "I'm in love with you. You're my everything." He wasn't sure what he wanted to do. He wasn't sure he wanted to try to get any closer.

But some of his online contacts were less romantic. He had friends online, and they just exchanged "Hey, what's going on?" kinds of messages. Jordan told me that he met younger guys online who only wanted some advice. He met older guys that would give him advice. It was a place he could hang out and talk with the other gay men.

Despite my doubts, I came to understand that this was his life, and there were many positives to his socializing this way.

I didn't advise him to stop what he was doing, but I did invite him to try to connect with people who lived near him. I suggested he use the gay apps, like Grindr, and start talking to people who weren't so far away.

He followed my advice, and soon he was having exchanges with people nearby, online romances, but also friendships. He'd get encouragement and support: "I'm rooting for you and glad you got the job" and like that.

Over time and continuing in therapy, he did move on to meeting some of his online contacts. Some of them were catfish, and some were nice but not enough to be partner material. But he's still looking, and more and more willing to meet his online friends and lovers. So, his having a virtual social life was a great way for him to lay a foundation for meeting people, a way for him to practice the skills he needed to meet people face-to-face.

Jordan's story isn't over. This is his second year of working with me. He hasn't met Mr. Right yet, but he's still looking. In the meantime, he has two or three "real" gay friends that he can do things with around town.

Don't Let Fear Control You

Many clients say they knew a boyfriend was stringing them along, or seeing other men, while telling them otherwise. Yet they kept on seeing this same man for fear of having no one at all. Gay or straight, anyone who strings someone else along is self-centered, concerned only about himself, with little or no regard for others. The "pretty" guy preys on "victims" with low self-esteem, because he's confident that he won't be rejected. The very worst of this type is the sociopath who just likes to make trouble and watch people squirm.

Many gay men who fear they're too old and/or unattractive link up with a narcissistic man, because they believe they deserve no better.

When clients are dating, I always coach them to be direct and honest. It's hard enough to handle all the issues they must face during the dating process. Integrity isn't just a moral issue—it saves valuable time. If you're not really attracted to a man, let him know (in a kind way) that you're not interested. Yes, he might feel hurt, particularly if he likes you. But that's okay. Let *him* move on. Making him feel more "comfortable" by giving him a line ("I'll call you sometime" or "This could be a great friendship") and then never calling back could be more hurtful still. Not everyone gets a hint—so be direct.

If you want to attract a man of integrity, then it is important to behave like one yourself. Not only should you be alert to their behaviors matching their words, but make sure your own do, too. Be who you say you are. Follow your words with actions.

Anonymous sexual encounters offer you adventures in which you can try out new things, but so can dating—in emotional, risk-taking ways. You can get rejected on either playing field. But just as cruising helps to refine your hookup skills, each date lets you clarify your emotional goals.

While dating, I did all kinds of things I'd never have done otherwise. I went boating and camping with a guy who loved the outdoors. I'd never done those things before, but I found they were fun. Other men I dated showed me fine dining experiences, different ways to dress, and more rewarding ways to look at life. I learned about good wines. I learned that dating a man who was too much like me could be boring, even horrifying. I needed a calmer, homebody person, not an anxious, overextended social guy. Overall, I acquired the skills and confidence to maintain a rewarding relationship. Again, discover what works and what doesn't work—for *you*.

A List of Tips

I'll finish out this chapter with some tips that summarize what I've learned counseling gay men on their relationships.

1. Set aside your pride. Dating is not for the hypersensitive. Even if the guy isn't interested in you because of how you look, or how you are in bed, remember that's about him and his desires, not about you. Another guy may want you because of the very thing this guy doesn't care for. Recognize that nothing is personal. Assure yourself that there's nothing wrong with you.

2. Step out of your own way. Listen to the guy's judgments of you, remembering they're 90 percent about him. However, there may be some kernel of truth to what he's saying. Hear his words, whatever they may be, and decide for yourself what you think about them.

3. Never play games. If you're not sure where the relationship is heading, or what his intentions are, be direct: "I really like you and would like to see more of you," or "When two men go out, it's hard to know if it is a date. I'd like this to be. Would you?"

4. Be vulnerable. With your feelings put aside and protected, you can allow yourself to take risks. Do and say things you

normally wouldn't. Use this as an opportunity to find out how you want to be in a relationship.

5. Don't let another guy play games or be indirect. Getting mixed signals? "You say this, but you do that. It confuses me. Can you tell me how you feel about me?" If, after some dialogue, he won't be direct, then he's not the guy for you.

6. Never judge either of you as right or wrong, good or bad. When dating isn't going well, it's easy and common for people to want to make things black and white. This is a dead-end road. Everyone has his own way of communicating and his own level of awareness, as you'll discover as you date different men. If that dating situation isn't working out for you, just move on to the next guy, without labeling anyone bad for being different.

7. Stay visible. Many of my clients struggle to find men to date because they're not involved in the gay community. Go to the LGBTQ community center, get on committees and boards, volunteer your time for gay organizations, help with a mailing, go to fundraisers. This is where active, confident gay men are.

8. Even if (especially if) things go badly, see dating as a fun experience, an adventure. This lesson was very hard for me. I dated lots of interesting characters for 10 years before I met my husband. Finally, during the last three years of dating, I let myself have fun—and learned a lot. Each guy I dated taught me something different and exposed me to new things in my life, for which I'm grateful.

9. Learn from each dating relationship. Observe yourself and reflect on what went well and what didn't. Were you open, honest, and direct? Did you hold back your thoughts and feelings just to make the relationship work? Were you moving too fast? Too slow?

10. Force yourself to approach men. Don't wait to be approached. If I approached a guy, especially in front of his friends, and struck up a conversation, it was worth the risk. How else would I ever know whether the encounter might turn into anything?

If the conversation didn't go well, I'd keep asking questions to break the ice. People like to talk about themselves. Being a therapist, I'm genuinely interested in learning about people.

But beware. Some men like to talk exclusively about themselves. If the conversation eventually does not move back to you, consider this a red flag. For many guys, everything you say about yourself becomes a prompt for something about themselves.

11. Go ahead and put ads on gay Internet websites and post on gay apps like Grindr, Scruff, and GROWLr. I've counseled lots of men who've found friends, dating partners, and long-term relationships that way. But don't forget about the catfish.

12. Learn to laugh about some of the experiences you are having. Laugh at yourself for the blunders you make.

Once, I dated a guy who drew stares wherever we went. At first I thought I was imagining it and asked whether he noticed it, too. He initially denied it, and later confirmed it, but he wouldn't say why. Was he on a wanted list? In the news for some scandal? Only later did I learn he was mayor of the city we were in. Because he'd lied about his job, I cut short our dating. Later, I couldn't stop laughing at the lengths he went to not to tell me.

Another time, I hosted a dinner party. During a quiet moment, a man I was dating told everyone he was a top. I was horrified. We hadn't yet had sex or even talked about it, but after that my guests must have assumed I was a bottom. While there is nothing wrong with that, I would rather they not know anything, verified or not, about me sexually.

The lesson: Laugh, then move on.

References

1. Sharon Kleinberg and Patricia Zorn. "Multiple Mirroring with Lesbian and Gay Couples: From Peoria to P-Town," in *Healing in the Relational Paradigm: The Imago Relationship Therapy Casebook*, edited by Wade Luquet and Mo Therese Hannah. Second edition. Washington, D.C.: Brunner-Routledge, 1998.

Chapter 9

Understand the Stages of Love

My partner and my father have the same name—DADDY!
—Comedian Eddie Sarfaty

Jokes like this make us laugh because we know there's a truth behind them. And unless you take those truths seriously, they can interfere with your ability to find and keep a relationship.

Straight or gay, we all long for contact and connection with one another. We yearn to be in lasting, adult love relationships. My clients and my friends talk constantly about their longings and yearnings to find a significant other. "With no partner," they say, "my life isn't complete." Of course, you'll hear the same remarks from our heterosexual counterparts.

But gay men who want to find a partner have a few extra hurdles and barriers.

Gay Couplehood

When my clients go to gay bars and social events and see an overwhelming majority of single—or at least seemingly unattached—men, they conclude that gay couplehood is rare, if not impossible. At clubs, at marches—even at my weekend workshops and therapy groups—single gay men are far more visible than partnered gay couples. This leads to the logical but totally inaccurate assumption that gay couples simply don't exist.

Compared with the heterosexual community, where romantic and married couples are more easily identified in public, gay relationships—short or long-term—are not nearly so visible.

Ironically, gay men are regularly accused of being promiscuous. Yet, when we want our monogamous relationships to be valued and legalized, we're told that we're wrong for even asking. Despite the 2015 Supreme Court ruling, gay marriage is hardly accepted by everyone everywhere in our society.

One night, back when I was single, I'd just ended a short relationship. I returned home from a gay bar, still reeking of tobacco smoke, partially deafened by the loud music, and feeling fairly depressed. A well-meaning family member was there to greet me. After I told her of my hopelessness about finding Mr. Right, she offered me some advice: "Maybe you'll meet lots of men and have multiple relationships throughout your life. Just enjoy the good times with them. When they end, expect it and move on."

At the time, her remark made me feel nurtured and comforted. Over time, however, I came to understand her words as products of ignorance and homonegativity. I couldn't imagine her "reassuring" my sister by telling her, "Maybe you'll have many boyfriends and husbands throughout your life. Just enjoy each one. When it ends, move on."

What I needed to hear was exactly what a heterosexual person needs to hear: "Hey. Don't worry. Mr. Right *is* out there. In fact, there are quite a few Mr. Rights, and you can settle down with one—if that's really what you want. The bars aren't the best place to meet someone. Keep trying, and go to more social events that aren't bar-related. You deserve fidelity and true love."

That's what I needed to hear that night, and that's what I want gay men to get from this chapter.

Support from Family and Friends

Our society tends to see relationships, gay and straight alike, as disposable. More than half of heterosexual marriages end in divorce. When a relationship runs into trouble, many participants decide to abort it and try for a better one. You'll get more support to leave a relationship than to stay in one. There are countless instances where disapproving parents wait for the first whiff of trouble, then use it as an excuse to challenge their heterosexual son's or daughter's commitment to a partner whom they never really liked in the first place. For gay relationships, that goes double.

Those who hear about marital counseling and couples therapy say, "Relationships shouldn't be so much work." But relationships, especially the good ones, are a *lot* of work. The idea that any problem indicates a bad relationship isn't true—except when serious emotional issues are involved and the partner won't seek treatment. For example, when violence or drug addiction are the problem, you need to seek a therapist for immediate help. You shouldn't have to put up with abuse.

Understanding What Relationships Really Are

Are you looking for Mr. Right or Mr. Right Now? So many of my clients talk about wanting a partner, but their efforts and behaviors don't reflect that. They actually do all they can to avoid seeing someone long-term. They want a relationship, but on an unconscious level, they see the work involved as scary, if not terrifying.

We can blame failed relationships on society, families, and friends all we want, but the bottom line is that we have to look within ourselves. Relationships force us to look at the darkest parts of who we are—as well as the most loving parts that exist in us, too.

Far too many gay men enter adult love relationships with the unspoken, internalized conviction that they themselves are inherently damaged and flawed. Their self-doubt becomes a self-fulfilling prophecy, and they project their own perceived weaknesses onto their partners. Meanwhile, there's also that imprinted expectation, conscious or not, that gay relationships won't last. Is it any wonder that when problems arise, they're taken as fatal flaws?

Few of us realize that problems are *supposed* to happen in a relationship and that they can speed us to great personal healing. For the physical body, moderate stress—as in brisk walking— helps leg bones stay solid and healthy. Just so for a relationship. Problems, properly dealt with, can help the bond strengthen and grow.

Imago Relationship Therapy

As a therapist, the most important training I ever received was Imago Relationship Therapy (IRT) as developed by Harville Hendrix. In *Getting the Love You Want: A Guide for Couples*, Hendrix outlines the stages of love and describes what attracts us to potential partners in the first place.[1] Many relationship books, like John Gray's *Men are from Mars, Women are from Venus*, focus on differences between men and women. Hendrix emphasizes the individual and not gender, which makes his model perfect for LGBTQ relationships as well as heterosexual ones.

Imago is the Latin word for image. Each of us assembles inside our minds a representation of an ideal person created from both the positive and negative traits of our mother, father, and any other primary caretaker we had when we were growing up. This becomes the model of the type of person we want to partner with in a committed, intimate relationship. We (usually unconsciously) project this ideal onto prospective partners, to see if they fit. Hendrix uses the word "Imago" for this "image" that we develop in childhood and use as a template for the rest of our lives.

Parts of our Imago can also be assembled from the community we grew up in, the religion we were taught, and from any important teacher, coach, or institution that left a profound impact on us while we were growing up. This composite image becomes a kind of treasure map that directs our search for adult love. We seek what feels familiar and therefore "safe"—even if it might seem exotic to someone else. Therefore, we look for someone who reminds us of both the best and the worst traits of our parents and primary caretakers.

Our unconscious tendency to choose partners that match our Imago can be turned to a useful therapeutic purpose. IRT teaches that we partner to heal ourselves and to complete the unfinished business of childhood. Because our original wounding—and for gay men, that includes heterosexism and homophobia—occurred in relationships with the people who raised us, our healing must also occur in the context of relationships, too.

Some people have difficulty with that concept because "wounding" feels too strong. I always ask them whether "negative influencing" fits better. Others feel that they did not have any childhood wounding at all. I tell them to pick up any Developmental Psychology 101 book and see all the developmental tasks one has to go through to survive childhood. No one escapes without some negative influencing. Simply having a younger sibling can create difficulties, because when he or she came along, you were no longer the Number One Child. Parents cannot raise a child perfectly; how their actions and decisions impacted us shows up later in our relationships.

Of course, you're not aware of these unconscious processes. You see a guy you're attracted to and say to yourself, "Wow, he is hot! I like his smile, his butt, his whatever." Meanwhile, your unconscious mind is saying, "Wow, familiar love! That's someone who reminds me of my Mommy and Daddy. I'm going over there."

If you ever want to prove this phenomenon, just talk to any adult child of an alcoholic. He'll tell you that there can be 499 sober people in a room and he'll zero in on the one alcoholic. That person hardly has to say a word for the child of an alcoholic to feel an attraction.

Imagine that your childhood was like a Broadway smash hit that ran year after year. However, when the play went on the road, the original cast had to be replaced. The script remained the same, but the actors who played the leads and acted out the story were entirely different people. When we grow into adulthood and take our "show" on the road, we choose partners, friends, and even coworkers who can take over the roles of our mothers, fathers, ex-partners, and siblings to help us recycle our childhood, for better and for worse.

For years, I've heard women—both in therapy and in conversation—complain that every man wants to be married to his mother. Well, in theory, being gay solved that problem for me! I knew I didn't want to be married to my mother or anyone like her, so I thought I was exempt. In my relationships with men, I suspected that more than likely, I'd have to deal with my father (with whom I didn't have a great relationship). Not so. In our Imago searching, gender is not the issue. I picked a man who carries the positive and negative traits of both my mother and father.

Of course, it's the negative traits of your more dominant parent—the one who affected you most—that most interfere with your adult relationships. This is because you'll find yourself seeking to resolve issues from your childhood in those relationships. You will naturally find a facsimile of your mother and father in a man who will provoke you like your mother and father did, but the goal of IRT is to lead your partner to be willing to modify his behavior to stop re-wounding you, in other words, to help you heal and resolve your past.

Again, our participation in this grand drama is all unconscious. However, the more you know about the process, the more mindful you become, and the better choices you make in selecting a partner. If you are already with another man, this realization can come as a great relief. When conflict arises, it's natural to assume that you're with the wrong person. Not so.

The *right* partner learns to change with you, knowing that this willingness to change will help him as well. Imago theory teaches that our partners hold the blueprint for our own personal growth and vice versa. What we need most from our partners is hardest for them to give us, because the very thing we are asking them for is often connected to their own greatest wounding.

For example, an Imago therapist I know, Joan, told me about how her lecturing and teaching around the country took her away from her husband and made her feel isolated and detached. Joan asked him if he'd be willing to call her every day during the one month she was gone. He resisted, saying, "My schedule is too busy."

But she told him that she felt ignored and neglected and that it would be healing for him do this for her, for just that one month. Ultimately he agreed; he called Joan every day to tell her he missed her and loved her. She began to feel more emotionally secure with him and, toward the middle of the month, thanked him for gifting her with his calls. Eventually she no longer needed them.

"But I don't want to stop," he replied. "I like calling you every day. It makes me feel more connected to you, as well."

He also was recovering a missing piece of his childhood intimacy that he never would have recovered otherwise. This is why it's important to be as attentive to your partner's needs as he is to yours. You both can benefit by giving each other what the other needs most.

Mike and I met in 1993. I'd had some short-term dating relationships that had lasted no longer than three or four months, and I didn't know what I was doing wrong. I'd been in therapy myself, been trained as a therapist, and still couldn't identify why I couldn't find Mr. Right. With earlier Imago training, maybe I could have spared myself some years of turbulence. I'd meet men who were narcissistic and inconsiderate—self-absorbed bully types. Yet, they didn't need to say a word for me to feel their energy and be drawn to them. I would tell myself, "It was his looks."

Now, I know there was more to it. Every time I started dating one of these men, to whom I was wildly attracted, he'd tell me how angry I was. I'd respond by saying that *he* was the one making me so angry, and if he'd just change his behavior, I'd calm down.

Ultimately—obviously—this scenario wouldn't work, and one of us would end the relationship.

From what I've learned in IRT, I now understand why I was drawn to these bullies. First, while I was growing up, boys in school taunted and humiliated me. I never stood up for myself because I didn't know how. I just took it. No one taught me how to protect myself. My parents divorced when I was three, and because of my father's absence and neglect, I was left with just my mother, who was the more dominant of the two. At home, her motto was, "My way or the highway." Again, I chose to acquiesce. My sister didn't, and our mother punished her regularly for not complying. So these narcissistic types I dated were quite right: Yes, I was angry. But they didn't deserve my level of anger, because it wasn't meant for them. It was unresolved rage toward my mother and father and those childhood bullies.

Relationships Are Triggers

In relationships, we regress to a time when we children were taught to be quiet and to accept whatever our larger, stronger counterparts dished out. We don't know this on a conscious level, so we assume that any problems we experience arise from the current relationship. In most cases, the relationship simply triggers memories and unresolved issues from a bygone time.

If our parents wounded us (or otherwise negatively influenced us), then they are the ones who can best help us to heal most deeply. However, a primary love partner who matches their traits can serve as their stand-in. Healing takes place when the partner we select says, in effect, *I can see I've hurt you and, unlike your parents, I'm willing to modify my behavior.*

In my case, if any of those self-absorbed men I dated had been willing to say, "Joe, sorry I disappointed you. I can see your point and am willing to consider your needs more," then I could have started to heal the pain from my childhood. Mike, my husband, was the first man I dated who finally did this, and he grabbed my heart.

Mark and Barry, both in their early 30s, had been together as a couple for six years. They came to see me for therapy because neither felt safe about sharing his feelings with the other. This is a common problem for couples: When communication breaks down, safety and trust diminish.

Mark came from a family of lower socioeconomic status. When he was young, his father abandoned the family, leaving Mark's mother to raise him and his two siblings. She dated violent men who would beat her. When Mark was 11 years old, one of her boyfriends stabbed another man in his presence.

Money was tight, and his mother worried constantly about how to pay the bills. Many nights she would stay out, leaving Mark, the oldest, to care for the other two children. Since his father was gone, being the "man of the house" made him feel privileged and important. His mother often called him her "little man." He was determined to comply with her wishes and not to give her any more concerns—and in doing so, denied the violence around him.

From a very young age, Mark knew he was gay and figured that becoming the "best little boy" would be a great cover. His mother would never notice—or even question—his sexuality. Consequently, Mark never said *no* to his mother and never learned to build appropriate boundaries.

Barry's mother died when he was very young. His older brother was detached, kept to himself, and resisted any contact with Barry. His father, a compulsive gambler, would sneak out of the house in the middle of the night to play poker. Later, Barry's father married a woman who was maternal and loving toward Barry, and whom he began to consider a mother figure. But she and Barry's father didn't get along. One day she told Barry she was divorcing his father and left. Once again, he felt abandoned and fearful.

Early on, he'd learned to take care of himself and not to trust people. When he'd formed strong attachments, the most important people in his life had abandoned him. Later, as you can guess, he often entered relationships with men who would suddenly leave him—giving Barry no clue as to why.

In therapy, Mark claimed that Barry was making too many demands of him. If he didn't do things the way Barry wanted, he felt that Barry became unreasonable. For his part, Barry felt frustrated because when Mark was upset, he wouldn't admit it. Barry would find out only later, when a quick, effective solution was no longer possible.

Mark stated that Barry should "just know" his needs, without having to be told. But Barry couldn't know, of course—and, weeks after the event had passed, he would feel blindsided by Mark's anger. Then, unfortunately, Barry would sweep his own feelings under the carpet, fearing that if he showed his hurt and confusion, Mark might abandon him. This was their core argument. They fought over different situations, but it always came down to the same issue: Mark felt Barry was too demanding, and Barry didn't realize when he'd upset Mark.

I offered them the Imago explanation of how past conflicts often get recycled in adult relationships—usually in disguised forms. I showed Mark how he projected a childhood wish onto Barry by assuming that Barry should intuit his needs without being told.

You Should Just Know

This is a common issue in relationships, gay and straight alike. I often hear one partner tell the other, "I shouldn't have to tell you. You should just know."

I always warn that this is dangerous. The only time you shouldn't have to tell someone your specific needs is in childhood—infancy in particular. As adults, we must explain our needs, preferences, and priorities. Otherwise, how—short of detective work or ESP—can our partners ever understand us?

Mark had to verbalize his own needs first, then get Barry to meet them. He also needed to set boundaries for himself and speak up when he felt that Barry was making too many demands. Neither of these was a skill he'd learned in childhood. Mark's mother was emotionally and often physically unavailable, which had kept him busy meeting everyone's needs but his own. Consequently, he tried to get his partner to give him what his mother never did. The problem was that his partner could not know his needs unless Mark articulated them.

Burdening your partner with meeting *all* of your unmet childhood needs is of course inappropriate; nevertheless, it is normal for most of us to try. Understanding this typical process helped Mark to identify his own needs and to communicate them to Barry—who became compassionate when he realized Mark's silences stemmed from his childhood. Barry saw he was simply triggering a sensitivity (a psychological "allergy," if you will) that Mark had developed long ago. The problem wasn't Barry's fault, as he originally thought (and as Mark had told him).

For his part, Barry learned that he was recycling the pain of losing two women he'd been very attached to—his mother and stepmother—and the neglect of his distant, gambler father. Barry kept his fears of conflict and abandonment to himself, dealt with them internally, and didn't communicate them to Mark. To make their relationship work, Barry's challenge was to risk voicing his needs and to face his fears that Mark might leave him.

Now that Mark understood where Barry's trauma had originated, he was more understanding and reassured Barry that a passing conflict wouldn't make him want to break up. As you can imagine, these insights were wonderfully liberating for them both. Barry and Mark started creating safety for each other. Their communication improved, and their connection to each other deepened.

Shadow Work

Unconsciously, we don't just seek partners who match our caretakers. We also search for people who display parts of ourselves that we have denied or disowned. Thus, your "ideal" partner may mirror aspects of yourself that are missing, distorted by defenses, and—at least for now—consciously lost.

When I met Mike, I immediately loved how peaceful and calm he was—so different from what I'd grown up with. I come from a very bold, forthright family. Everyone says whatever's on his or her mind, with no regard for others' feelings. Around them, I never knew when an argument was going to break out. Had I been quiet and easygoing, I'd have been bulldozed—so my tranquil, placid side went into hiding.

But Mike's family wasn't emotional and demonstrative. In me, he recognized the part of himself that yearned to argue or show strong emotion. He'd tell me, "You are so passionate, vibrant, and alive." So our lost parts met each other, along with familiar love from our childhood caretakers. We mirrored each other's Imago without even knowing it.

This is "Shadow work" in the language of Carl Jung and Robert Bly. My peaceful self was in shadow, as was Mike's emotional self. Our two Shadows met and came out of hiding into the light.

Romantic Love

The goal of Imago Therapy is to establish committed, conscious, intimate relationships by aligning the conscious mind (which usually seeks happiness and good feelings) with the agenda of the unconscious mind, which seeks healing and growth. I love that IRT puts a positive spin on relationship problems that otherwise seem impossible.

Almost all of us enter relationships through the wide, splendid gateway of *romantic love*. Movies, books, television, and pop music all celebrate the infatuation period when all the lights are on. Every positive detail is vivid and visible. It all feels so great.

For LGBTQ individuals, this is a time of even greater importance. It's when we realize we have found something (more precisely, someone) that we were told we couldn't ever have. We feel so lucky, fulfilled, and finally authentic. We've waited a lifetime for a connection like this. We don't want it to end. During this stage, which our society calls "real love," everyone—gays, lesbians, bisexuals and straights alike—reports feelings of elation, exhilaration, and euphoria.

Three archetypal feelings offer a glimpse into the unconscious realm of romantic love:

1. "I know we just met, but I feel I've always known you." People feel this way because their unconscious minds have selected a partner with positive and negative traits which match those of their childhood caretakers. Because your unconscious doesn't know the difference between past and present, you really do feel you've "always" known him.

2. "When I'm with you, I feel whole and complete." We feel whole when we meet someone who expresses the "lost" parts of ourselves that have been disowned or denied.

3. "I can't live without you." This is an unconscious transfer of responsibility for our very survival from our parents to a partner. Unconsciously, we fear that if the partner leaves, we'll lose our lives. It's a primitive feeling. Children know that if their parents abandon them, they can't survive. But in adulthood, the unconscious mind doesn't recognize the difference when a partner leaves.

These three archetypal feelings are strongest when both partners are physically together. During this time, they can operate on less sleep, as if they're on stimulants. Indeed, during this time, infatuated people will say they feel drugged. If they've been depressed before, they now report being less so. If they suffer from addictions, they'll experience diminished craving or even feel "cured." Their sex drive will tend to match their partner's.

There's literally some chemistry in what's going on here. The experience of falling in love produces natural chemicals similar to amphetamines—dopamine, norepinephrine and especially phenylethylamine (PEA).[2] When you're in (romantic) love, you actually *are* drugged, without realizing it. The first time this cocktail of chemicals is released, it has its greatest effect, which is why people never forget their first love. Problem is, each time it is released, it's less powerful, and its effect lasts for a shorter period of time. It's not meant to last. Its only biological purpose is to connect two otherwise incompatible people, bond them, and make them willing to stay together.

Many gay men seek nothing beyond the falling-in-love high. After it wears off, they complain that a relationship shouldn't be "so much work," and they're off to a new man. With heterosexual couples, by the time the love chemistry wears off, they are often engaged, with marriage and children following soon after. Not that these are the best of reasons to stay in a relationship, but they are factors that help heterosexual couples stay committed. Gay men usually don't have these same anchors to keep them steadfast.

Even so, infatuation isn't real love, much less "true." It's only nature's way of bringing two humans together. It's supposed to happen—but also, for gays and straights alike—it's supposed to come to an end. (Most straight people don't know this, as you can see from the divorce statistics.) And when it does end, sometimes that seems to confirm a gay man's worst fears about love.

Too often, we enter a relationship with the belief that heterosexual relationships are superior and that gay relationships don't last. So when a gay romance does end, it seems like a confirmation of the myth that love and romance are reserved for heterosexuals only and that gays cannot enjoy lasting love.

No one tells us that this phenomenon is universal. Romantic love is supposed to end—for everyone. PEA and its fellow love drugs only makes staying together easier at first—before the necessary work begins.

Even so, when lightning strikes, many gay men do everything they can to hang onto the man who inspired it. Gay partners sometimes break up and get back together many times, because their reunion triggers a fresh dose of PEA. After a period of absence, both recall the thrill of their first meeting and say, "Let's do it again!"

One way men—gay, bisexual and straight—try to maintain this romantic high is by having (though not necessarily enjoying) sex outside of the relationship. The sheer thrill of the hunt generates a new jolt of chemicals, which they can then bring back home. Still another way to recharge the PEA high is to invite other sex partners into the relationship.

The Power Struggle

The next stage in a relationship after romantic love is the *power struggle*. It has a finite duration—thankfully, because this phase doesn't feel so good. Your chemically induced rose-colored glasses fall off; your perceptions "return to normal." If you were depressed before, you return to your depressed state. If you enjoyed a higher than normal sex drive, you revert to your normal libido. You become acutely aware of the differences between yourself and your partner, differences that PEA made seem trivial and unimportant. You feel profoundly disillusioned. Unaware that this progression out of romantic love is natural and inevitable, you tend to blame yourself—or your partner—for the collapse of your romantic bliss.

Most people become aware of the power struggle when various kinds of issues of commitment arise. Imagine one member of the couple saying to the other (listed in ascending order of commitment):

1. "Let's buy something together."
2. "Let's only see each other and stop dating other people."
3. "Let's take a vacation together."
4. "Let's move in together—or talk about the possibility."
5. "Let's get married [or engaged]."

The romantic stage brings on closeness, but once you're close, issues of dependency and commitment arise. You will typically fight for your choices over your partner's choices, your way over his way. In other words, fear of being dependent, of being committed, brings on a struggle for power.

When Mike and I started talking about living together (before I knew about Imago) we immediately started fighting. Where were we going to live? What furniture would be in the house? I'm not superficial or materialistic, but all of a sudden these details mattered to me—enormously. He wasn't going to let go of his vision, and neither was I. Even though we argued about furniture and housing, those weren't the real problem.

Mike and I kept arguing about chairs and sofas until we got to the root of the problem. I was raised in a family where, in order to

survive, I had to set aside my sense of self. So when Mike
suggested that I move into *his* house with *his* possessions, I was
transported back to a time when I was told that my needs didn't
matter. That wasn't at all what Mike was saying to me, but I was
unknowingly projecting that onto him. I became defensive and
fought back. I hadn't been able to do that in childhood, but now I
could argue for my needs, and that's exactly what I did. I
consciously thought the issue was about the house and furniture,
but unconsciously it was much more important. It was about my
sense of self.

Luckily, we started Imago Therapy at this time and came to a
realization of what was happening; in particular, the important
unconscious issues that underlay our conscious and superficial
disagreements.

Once I understood, I pushed for my needs in other ways and
encouraged Mike to meet them with compassion and
understanding. He realized our conflict was not about him at all but
came from another time in my life, which helped him see my point
of view.

Fortunately, we discovered the real issue in time for us to
work it out. Many others are not so lucky and break up without
ever learning what they were really arguing about.

Couples often argue over things that are not the core issue.
The unconscious finds a way to disguise the real problems with
more innocuous, seemingly unimportant matters. But they feel
very, very important! The power struggle, then, is the second stage
of relationships. Many couples never reach the end of the power
struggle, because they don't know how to navigate their way
through it.

The context of the power struggle is *coded material*. When
you decipher it, you'll find information to help you to know
yourselves better—as individuals and as a couple.

Most of the emotions we attach to any problem are connected
to the past. Once you and your partner see that, you both will be
more willing to address the situation in a more positive spirit.

In romantic love, our similarities connect us. The love-chemical cocktail helps us bond—for a while. But during the power struggle we're disconnected by the very differences we thought we could overlook. Nature gave us help in the romantic stage but dropped us off without a guidebook during the power struggle.

The power struggle begins in earnest with the realization that your partner can't or won't meet all your needs, as you originally expected. (Back in the romantic love phase, he may even have promised to do so.) And so old hurts and resentments reawaken. Mostly, these are old hurts from childhood, but they can also arise from unresolved conflicts from past relationships.

During the power struggle stage, you'll hear statements like: "You know what I need. I don't have to tell you, and I shouldn't have to." or, "You have what I need, but you won't give it to me."

After the romantic period ends, of course, sex drives fall back to normal. The person with the higher libido may say, "You were more sexual when we first met. It was just a ploy to get me to move in with you." In other words, *You have what I need, and you won't give it to me.* This "what I need" usually reflects some childhood need that went unmet—not sex, of course, but usually attention and responsiveness from a caregiver.

During the romantic stage, we begin to feel a sense of entitlement to whatever we want from our partner, as if he owes us. (Again, this is a regression to the blissful days of infancy, when an ideal caregiver was quick to answer our every complaint.) Now, we find that our partner is different from what we thought—and for that, of course, we blame him. The very things that attracted us become things we dislike. Qualities we once adored, we cannot bear.

If we've repressed any parts of ourselves, keeping them in Shadow, we can tolerate them in a partner for only a short while. Then, we seek to "kill off" these traits, which we recognize in the partner but not in ourselves. All too often, the relationship is the first victim.

You'll recall how I loved Mike's calmness and serenity. During our power struggle, I asked him things like, "Are you alive in there? Don't you ever feel anything?" At the start, he loved my passion, but soon he complained, "You're too emotional." He'd retreat to another room, and I'd follow, demanding that we work things out. He was afraid of my insistence, and I was afraid of his walking away—out of fear of abandonment. As many others do, I assumed that by unleashing a verbal hailstorm I could coerce Mike into communicating. Instead, he'd become a turtle and withdraw into his shell.

The Turtle and the Hailstorm

In most relationships, one partner plays the turtle and the other the hailstorm. One pulls inward, and the other explodes—verbally and emotionally. (And depending on the issue, quite often the two partners can switch roles.) Hailstorms can seem scarier, because they're loud and energetic. But to a hailstorm, a turtle's retreat can be just as scary—making the hailstorm feel abandoned and threatened. And sometimes, the turtle can become a snapping turtle. (Harville Hendrix created this metaphor. I use it at workshops, where it usually helps people lighten up about this common power struggle.)

Many people feel that conflict is a relationship's kiss of death. But few of us—and gay men especially—realize that this dynamic is healthy. What's *not* healthy is how most people deal with it.

Yes, getting through the power struggle is very difficult. But it's the entry point to real love. It may seem easier to break off the relationship, to have an affair, or to engage in addictive behavior, rather than face your deepest conflicts and fears. The good news is that the power struggles you face with your partner actually suggest that you're with the right person for your maximum growth. You have met someone who will challenge you to make necessary changes in yourself—which can only benefit the two of you. It's an opportunity to develop closeness and intimacy while still maintaining your individuality.

Conflict Is Growth Trying to Happen

Conflict enables you to differentiate yourself from your partner, to establish boundaries, and eventually to flourish as a couple. For us LGBTQ people, who've spent our entire lives trying to conform and disown who we really are, keeping that sense of self in a relationship is even more difficult.

Differences can be very threatening to any couple, but particularly to gay partners. Because society judges gay men as "different," we assume that differences are not okay, which, in turn, makes gay men wary of having to conform to anyone else's standards. But, after all, isn't this what we want from our families and from society as a whole: To be who we are, to let everyone else be who they are, and to allow differences without making them into conflicts?

Again, I am not talking about differences which are abusive. If you are in relationship with a man who will not take responsibility or be accountable for his own behaviors, and blames you for most or all of the problems, that is about disrespect and lack of integrity on his part, not "differences." Serious emotional problems or drug addictions cannot be addressed by Imago Therapy, but must be treated with specialized recovery programs.

Each year in the fall, with the holidays approaching, I ask gay couples about their plans. They often speak about going home to their separate families, without each other. I always tell clients that they hired me to be controversial and challenging, so I question and challenge this—not to make them uncomfortable, but to shake things up. I want to explore whether this holiday pattern represents any internalized homophobia (it usually does). Often, I ask the couple whether they can imagine their parents going to holiday functions without each other. We all usually laugh that they might *want* to do it, but don't.

Most heterosexual couples take turns going every other year to the other family (or to both on that same day), and they go together. To gay couples, I point out that not doing so sends a message to their families and to themselves that they aren't united, or that the relationship isn't as real as the marriages of their heterosexual siblings and family members. This only weakens their relationship.

At these moments, ask yourself: Is your commitment to your partner or your family? The "family" option drains intimacy from your relationship. Straight boys and girls commit to partners their parents don't approve of, so why should we be any different? But when you and your partner discuss a joint decision to boldly show your parents and siblings your commitment to each other, you typically must face the power struggle. It will naturally come up, because insisting that your relatives recognize you as a couple is a major step in the direction of commitment and dependence.

A family's failure to recognize their gay loved one's partnership as a valid relationship manifests in many ways. A gay son's family often views him as "single," even if he's partnered. When he doesn't have children, hasn't had a wedding ceremony, and fails to clearly present his relationship as a partnership of love, then his family may naturally choose to avoid the reality of their gay son's coupled status. Often, he sees his relationship as inferior to those of his married siblings and finds it difficult to stand up for himself. It's up to you to present yourself and your partner as a family unit.

Kenny and Brad had been together two years when they came to see me. Kenny was completely out to his family, but Brad wasn't out to his. They were having problems, because the year before he met Kenny, Brad ended a five-year relationship. At gatherings, Brad's family—not realizing the facts—constantly asked about Charlie, who to them was just a friend of Brad's who had come to all the past family functions. Kenny became angry at having to listen to Brad's family go on and on about how much they liked Charlie.

A straight man usually introduces the woman he's dating as his girlfriend. If they break up, he tells his family about it and introduces his next companion as his girlfriend, too. It's clear she's the new woman in his life—and families are usually tactful enough not to ask about his old flame in front of the new one. As a result of this conflict, Brad and Kenny's lines of communication had broken down, which diminished their feelings of safety and mutual trust.

After the three of us worked together for several months, their ability to communicate improved. Their connections to each other—and safety and trust—returned. But Kenny continued to express frustration about Brad's reluctance to tell his family that he was gay, that Kenny was his partner, and that they were a family unit.

Yes, "family" is definitely the word to use. (I often hear straight couples without children referring to themselves as families.) In the gay community, we couples call ourselves family to help people—and ourselves—recognize that there are all kinds of valid families. And a gay couple is one of them.

However, with the Christmas and Hanukah holidays approaching, I asked Brad and Kenny my usual question: "What are you going to do?" They replied that each would still visit his own family on his own. They also disclosed that neither family gave gifts to the other man's partner. Worse still, Brad's family continued to purchase gifts for Charlie every Christmas.

Ultimately, Brad decided it was time to come out to his parents. This was very difficult for him on various levels and for various reasons. But he knew that his relationship would only get stronger if he reinforced the idea that he'd started his own family.

I haven't worked with Brad and Kenny for a number of years, but recently I received an invitation to their wedding—to which they invited their friends and both their families. They had come a long way.

Your Partner Is Not Your "Friend"

Introducing your partner as a "friend" indicates that he's not special enough for you to tell the truth. And postponing this kind of challenge only means it will come back in a more powerful form.

At the talks I give to LGBTQ audiences, I strongly stress the importance of making partnerships clear to hosts who send invitations. It's inappropriate to say "and guest," or to use two separate invitations when inviting a couple. But it's up to you to inform whoever sends the invitations that you *are* part of a couple. It's not fair to assume they should know, and many people are simply unsure how to handle the situation.

If you're faced with such a dilemma, my advice is to call the sender and ask simply, "Please send the invitation to both of us."

When I was first partnered, I did exactly that. I sent out holiday cards from Mike and me—that is, from both of us. If one of my relatives sent me an invitation, I called to let them know that I was partnered, and that I'd like to bring Mike to the event. Next time, could they please invite us both? Some of my relatives were not okay with this, and then I would decline.

I knew up front that I was taking a risk. But simply knowing you're taking that risk makes the risk less risky. If Mike wasn't invited to an event, I wouldn't go either. That sent a strong message to my relatives—and to Mike—that we were now a family of our own. I wouldn't accept less respect than they would show a heterosexual couple.

Maya Kollman trained me to become a Certified Imago Relationship Therapist. In her article, "Helping Couples Get the Love They Want," she writes, "The Imago process is particularly useful for the LGBTQ community, because same-sex couples, who experience all the same typical ups and downs as opposite-sex couples, are expected to cope with these challenges without the same ample support systems straights have. Often, they feel isolated, as adrift on a desert island. Teaching them the Imago model is like offering these castaways the tools they need to build a paradise of connection."[3]

I love that notion. With so many negative influences bearing down on our relationships, we must find the support we need wherever we can. Both personally and professionally, I am deeply grateful for the Imago's optimistic, people-oriented model—one of the best therapeutic interventions to help our relationships evolve into mature love.

References

1. Harville Hendrix. *Getting The Love You Want: A Guide for Couples*. New York: Henry Holt and Company, 1988.
2. Anastasia Toufexis. "The Right Chemistry," *Time*, June 24, 2001.
3. Maya Kollman. "Helping Couples Get the Love They Want," *In The Family* magazine, April, 1997.

Chapter 10

Commit to a Partner

I wish you straight people would stop trying to prevent us from marrying each other. If you let us marry each other, then we will stop marrying you!

—Gay comedian Jason Stuart

When I heard that joke, my mind flashed to all my gay clients who have been heterosexually married. The heterosexually married gay man is in a bind. He's in a mixed marriage: He's gay, and she's straight. Thus the intensity of the couple's intimacy is limited. The connection between these two individuals is weak compared to the fulfillment he could have with another man and that she could have with a man who's thoroughly heterosexual.

Yet most formerly married gay men admit that in some ways, they were glad they'd married. They enjoyed all that went with it—their weddings, the birth of their children, family support, and a stable, secure home life. As married heterosexuals, they didn't have to worry about prejudice when their spouses telephoned at work, came to holiday parties, or gave them photographs to display on their desks. Typically, my heterosexually married gay clients worry that such satisfactions can't be recreated in gay culture.

As gay men, it's possible to have all that—though it involves a bit more work for us than for our heterosexual counterparts.

Everyone needs to understand that the more he commits to a partner, the harder their relationship becomes. But as you saw in the last chapter, the difficult parts can be positive and healthy. You just need to know how best to navigate through them.

Learning Relationship Skills from Women

Straight or gay, we all yearn to be in lasting love relationships. Gays are regularly assaulted with charges that we're promiscuous and that all we want is anonymous sex. We're the only minority that mainstream society criticizes for longing to be in committed relationships with others of our own culture.

Many of my gay clients who were once heterosexually married say that issues arising in their gay relationships are similar to ones they grappled with during their marriages to women. But now the issues are more intense. Being with someone of the same gender provides gay men with a better Imago match. The romance is more exhilarating—and the power struggle more acute. But they usually report that the exchange is well worth the hassle because they know they're with the right person.

Still, I have observed that heterosexually married gay men, and gay men who've enjoyed long-term friendships with women, seem to have absorbed some relationship skills not typical of men in general. If one or both partners have emerged from a heterosexual marriage, they tend to be more engaged in their current relationship. They're more compassionate, adaptable and accommodating.

Of the 22 participants at one of my Gay Men's Weekend Workshops, 18 were still in heterosexual marriages, were just ending them, or had ended them some time ago. Compared to other workshop participants, they were much more punctual. They showed more consideration for one another and for the workshop staff. They were mindful of the time they spent talking and sharing and, overall, showed a better understanding of the work involved. They simply had more empathy.

I think these skills were taught (if not demanded) by the women in their lives. Gay men who don't have this experience with straight women must learn these traits and techniques on their own.

Comparing Straight, Gay, and Lesbian Couples

When a gay client doesn't think gay men can commit deeply, I throw some facts his way. For over 30 years, John Gottman, a well-known psychologist, has worked with heterosexual couples and with gay and lesbian couples, too. His work is research-based, using observable, quantitative measurements. He brings couples to a "love lab"—essentially, a pleasant bed-and-breakfast. Each couple interacts with their partner, while hooked up to various machines that monitor their heart rates and perspiration levels.

Gottman's findings are an important, welcome addition to the chronicle of same-gender relationships. In his work with Robert Levenson, Gottman shows that gay and lesbian couples have some advantages over their heterosexual counterparts.[1] To determine why relationships succeed or fail, Gottman and Levenson assessed 21 gay and 21 lesbian couples over 12 years—based on direct observations of their expressions, and tones of voice, self-reports, interviews, and videotaped interaction. They compared these to a "control" group of 42 straight couples—a total of 84 couples, each together at least two years.

Gay couples were comparable to heterosexual couples in the quality of their relationships; they report the same happiness and satisfaction. Interestingly, gay couples weren't as prone to jealousy. If a straight guy says, "That woman's really hot," his wife will give him a hard time. If a woman comments on another man's nice "package" or "six-pack abs," the man in her life may feel hurt, and may or may not make a fuss. By contrast, two gay men can admire another man and comment on how attractive he is, but neither takes it personally or feels threatened.

Among heterosexual couples I've treated, women often feel that by commenting on another woman's good looks, their husbands literally cheat on them. Gay and lesbian couples may show some reactivity to such remarks, but usually much less.

Same-gender couples, Gottman and Levenson found, are much better at talking openly and honestly about their sex lives. In an article by Mubarak Dahir in *The Windy City Times*, Gottman remarked, "When we videotape a heterosexual couple talking about lovemaking, you have no idea what they are talking about."[2] We're of the same gender, with the same orgasmic reactions, timing, and sensations. Heterosexual couples have less understanding of each other and function differently.

Gottman and Levenson provide another eye-opener. Over their 12-year study, only 20 percent of the gay and lesbian couples broke up, compared to 38 percent of the heterosexual couples. At the study's end, almost twice as many straight couples were no longer together. In the face of adversity, gay and lesbian couples were much more optimistic. When addressing conflicts between them, they used more humor and affection.

Before leaving my office at the end of a session, lesbian couples generally hug each other. I've learned from that and encourage gay male couples to do the same. At the very least, one will crack a joke, and both will laugh—which can be just as effective. Only rarely have I been able to get heterosexual couples to do this after a session.

Gottman and Levenson also found that gay and lesbian couples take things less personally. I've found this more common with gay male couples. Gay men—again, because we're conditioned to behave like all other men—can shrug off an argument and not take it too much to heart. But I've spent countless hours of therapy trying to help lesbian couples not take things so *very* personally. On the other hand, gay males too often tend to shrug off arguments, and I must help them see things a little *more* personally to be sure that they'll work through important issues.

Teaching Men How to Talk to Each Other

Ted and David would get on Grindr and other gay apps looking for men who were interested in three-ways. David wasn't happy with this, but Ted insisted they do it. Eventually, David stopped trying to get Ted to see his point of view and just went along. I had to emphasize that looking for three-ways wasn't the problem—the problem was that David wasn't a consenting partner. He needed help to confront Ted's lack of interest in his personal feelings. Without my intervention, this behavior would have continued, with David and their relationship both suffering.

Luke and Tony let their dog sleep in their bed with them at night. It was actually Tony's idea. Both of them found it cute at first, but Luke began to feel uncomfortable. He'd want to cuddle or initiate sexual contact, only to find Tony cuddling with the dog. To have sex at night, they'd put the dog in another room, but he would whine and want to come in.

Luke tried to talk to Tony about this, but to no avail. Ultimately, he totally subordinated his emotional needs and let the issue drop. His job required a lot of travel away from home, so he rationalized that sharing their bed with the dog was "the least he could do for Tony," thereby minimizing the problem this sleeping arrangement caused their relationship. Again, I urged Luke to talk to Tony about his feelings and not to let the situation continue.

Gottman and Levenson observe that, "In a fight, lesbians show more anger, humor, excitement, and interest than conflicting gay men. This suggests that lesbians are more emotionally expressive—positively and negatively—than gay men. This may result from having two women in a relationship. Both have been raised in a society where expressiveness is more acceptable for women... " Their research revealed that gay male couples "aren't as adept in repairing relationships after negativity, during a fight... gay men may need extra help to offset the impact of negative emotions that inevitably come along when couples fight."[3]

In my practice I've also noted that male couples do tend to have difficulty getting over negativity after an argument. In relationships, the female usually pushes to talk directly and express feelings. Without her energy, these factors must be consciously brought into a gay male relationship. As a therapist, I often feel like the woman pushing gay men to appropriate these techniques into their relationships.

Male and Female Energy

Every couple I see has both male and female energy—even gay male couples. Female and male energies are more about what Western society *calls* feminine or masculine. For example, we think of women as homemakers and men as breadwinners. But plenty of men—straight and gay alike—prefer being homemakers. In our society, we call that feminine energy. But even if the male is a carrier of female energy, he doesn't necessarily have the skills that women have been socialized to possess.

There are usually more lesbian than gay couples at my workshops for couples. I take that to indicate that women are socialized to value relationships more. During check-in at one workshop, a lesbian couple said they were breaking up and had come to salvage their friendship. They reported that they'd spent 25 years together and wanted to leave with integrity, maintaining the strong connection they'd had before—only now, in a different way. I was impressed that they were so mature and respectful of their past relationship.

Again, there's nothing inherently gay or lesbian about this. It's strictly a male/female distinction. Women are encouraged to be in touch with their emotions, value close relations, and be considerate of the other people in their lives. Men are raised to be competitive, goal-oriented, sexually aggressive breadwinners who keep their emotions inside. As a result, many gay males overwork, focus on outer tasks rather than inner ones, have sex outside of their relationships, and seldom express emotions to their partners (or to themselves or anyone else, for that matter).

I've also noticed that most gay men are very capable of engaging in dialogue, being compassionate, and bonding emotionally with others. We're often much more in touch with our emotions than straight men, but in our adult love relationships, it's a whole different story. We haven't been encouraged to bond *deeply* with other men—in fact, just the opposite. Because of homophobia, we're taught from an early age not to hug or kiss other boys, express emotion to them, or talk to guys about our inner lives. We bring all this baggage, along with our family upbringing, into any love relationship.

Heading for the Exits

Harville Hendrix addresses the question of "exits": Behaviors that individuals use to remove themselves from relationships— emotionally and/or physically. In *Getting the Love You Want*, he writes, "An exit is acting out one's feelings rather than putting them into language."[4]

If you can't express anger toward someone, you'll inevitably act out the emotion in that person's absence. (The classic example is the man who, after his boss chews him out at work, comes home and kicks his dog.) Or else you'll act it out sideways through passive-aggressive behavior. If you find yourself doing this, it doesn't mean that you're a bad person, you're just scared and hesitant. Exits are simply ways of avoiding intimacy.

We all employ them—usually unconsciously. They arise most often when two people move from romantic love to the power struggle and come up against intimacy issues within the relationship. Exits reduce the power struggle's intensity and pain, basically by watering down the dependency in the relationship.

There are plenty of ways to get on an exit ramp. In the least extreme instances, they take the form of shopping, working out, devoting time to pets or relatives' kids, or pursuing a new hobby. What's wrong with these normal behaviors? Not the activities themselves, but the excessiveness that induces you to spend time away from your partner.

I often treat gay couples where one partner is over-involved in community service or work, or the other dotes on a pet, spends more time with his children than his partner, or gardens every daylight hour on the weekend. Often, the issue is overdoing social media. Maybe you've heard of "phubbing," snubbing someone in favor of a cell phone.

How can you distinguish reasonable activity from an exit? Either you must admit to yourself that you're using these activities to escape, or your partner must tell you. If I'm doing too many weekend workshops, my husband, Mike, taps me gently on the shoulder and says, "Another weekend away from me?" In the past, I used to tell him, "The gay community needs this. I have to do it." or, "This is my job." Both statements are true, but I had no idea how my being away so often was affecting us.

The point that Mike was making—which I finally got—wasn't that I needed to stop doing weekend workshops, but that I needed not to do them so frequently. Mike encouraged me to spend more time with him—which I needed and wanted to do. If he hadn't pointed this out, I wouldn't have realized how I was exiting our relationship.

Other exit strategies coincide with common troublemaking behaviors. For example, if a man constantly threatens to leave his partner, or tells himself he can always get out of the relationship— in short, if he thinks of breaking up before he gives the relationship a full chance—he unconsciously builds his partnership to resemble a mild form of divorce.

The exit impulse can also take the form of basic aggression, domestic violence, or emotional and verbal abuse. "Accidental" carelessness—a form of passive aggression—also fits here. We see this behavior in the man who forgets his partner's birthday or, worse, who cheats on him and comes home to have unprotected sex. Obviously, this puts the unsuspecting partner at great risk for various sexually transmitted diseases (STDs), including HIV. This can be lethal—not only to the relationship.

Less severe. but still destructive, are poor self-care (such as not getting regular medical checkups and not maintaining one's physical body through exercise) and passive indifference to emotional problems such as depression or anxiety. Untreated addictions also serve as effective exits. Is a man more committed to alcohol, drugs, sex, gambling, or food than to his partner? Again, addiction diminishes the intimacy that any relationship demands.

Some clients complain that their relationships literally drive them crazy. When I think of insanity, I prefer the concept used in 12-step groups: engaging in the same behaviors—doing the same thing over and over—and expecting different results. (I think cheating on one's partner while not engaging in safe sex is also a form of insanity. Even if putting him at risk isn't the exiting partner's intent, denying that possibility is insane.) I am not talking about psychotic insanity here, where a person hallucinates, is delusional, or loses touch with reality. In neurotic insanity, one is in touch with reality but engages in dangerous or destructive behaviors despite being aware of the possible consequences.

If you find yourself involved in one or more of these exits, it's very important that you not begin to think of yourself as a bad person. These behaviors simply indicate trouble in your relationship or within yourself. You (or with your partner, as a couple) need professional help.

Harville Hendrix talks about the "no exit decision." To commit more fully to your relationship, you must begin a discussion about closing off your exits. We recognize that not all exits can be closed that easily. So a more appropriate expectation is a "no exit *discussion*." For instance, if your partner's drinking too much or doing drugs, you and he can begin to talk about the effects of his behavior on your relationship. Then solutions, healing, and re-entry into intimacy can begin as energy starts moving away from whatever exits he's engaged in.

Closing exits is a process, not an event. It can take a while to close an exit—usually the exit's there for a reason, to meet a need or avoid a hurt. Whatever the reason, you should address it, bring it to consciousness, and examine how it's impacting you and your partner. Just discussing it with him brings energy back into your relationship.

Many people enter partnership with their exits already up and running. Many addictions and mood disorders like depression or anxiety lie dormant prior to a relationship. During the relationship they may surface or worsen in response to the demand for intimacy. This is not the result of a bad relationship, but rather an opportunity to look at why you engage in intimacy avoidance behaviors and to look at what it means to have a deep level of intimacy in your life.

Exits are mostly the result of the conflict between your desire to be with a partner and your fear of being in a relationship. The more you commit, the more childhood feelings, memories, and experiences tend to surface, because you have increased your dependency onto your partner. For many of us, saying "I want intimacy" or "I want a relationship" is frightening. The more abusive and traumatic your childhood, the greater your fear of committing yourself. Going back there is really scary.

Because gay boys were taught early on to avoid other gays, pursuing another man goes directly against that imprint. We manage the problem in different ways. Creating exits in our relationships lets us tolerate the closeness that troubles us. Our conscious "adult" side says, "Nothing to be afraid of. I'm in the relationship of my dreams!" But our unconscious, emotional side says, "This is childhood all over again. I feel endangered!"

The Intentional Couples Dialogue

Commitment is difficult. The more we commit, the deeper the power struggle, which raises more conflict. If problems remain unresolved, our relationship no longer feels emotionally safe. Communication breaks down. Distrust sets in. This becomes the natural state of dysfunctional relationships. This is where couples usually are when they come to me.

Imago Relationship Therapy has a wonderful communication exercise that I use with most every couple—actually, it's the foundation of all Imago techniques. This "Intentional Couples Dialogue" has three parts: Mirroring, validation, and empathy. It offers couples ways to communicate through dialogue, not monologue.

When our partner tries to convey a message, most often we're waiting our turn—not truly listening. We sit in our own reactivity, not truly hearing our partner's voice. This is monological communication.

By contrast, dialogue involves mirroring. One partner sends information, on one topic, until he's entirely finished, in short declarative sentences starting with "I." The receiver doesn't interpret, diminish, or magnify the message, but simply reflects what's said until the sender says, "There's no more."

Deceptively simple. But therapists do it all the time. You'd learn these basic reflective listening skills in an emergency crisis center. Carl Rogers, a well-known psychologist, found people felt more connected and understood when therapists used these reflective listening techniques. It was brilliant for Hendrix to suggest that partners use it with one another.

What did your partner say? "I'm upset that you don't appreciate it when I clean up." As the receiver, you say, "You don't feel I appreciate your cleaning up the house. And you're upset?" Then you add, "Did I get it? Is there more?"

This doesn't stop until the sender feels heard and understood.

Saying *Did I get it?* sends the message that you're really trying to understand what your partner's saying. *Is there more?* tells him that your ears are open and you *do* want to hear.

The second part of intentional dialogue is validation. After your partner finishes speaking, you validate what you heard, from *his* point of view. For most people, this is difficult. You respond, "What you're saying makes sense. I can see why you'd think this way." This isn't necessarily agreement—you're simply validating your partner's point of view. You look through his eyes to affirm the way he views the world. Yours isn't the only way to view conflicts in your relationship!

Because we gays and lesbians have been told over and over that what we think and feel is wrong, validating can be hard. Saying to someone, "That makes sense" can feel like a stretch, especially when you don't agree. In our society, we assume that what makes one person right makes another wrong.

The last part of the technique is empathy. Imagine what your partner might be feeling, given what he's said. You validate not just his words but his *feelings*. We men aren't taught to do this as well as women, so, as a therapist, I spend lots of time helping men learn to be empathic with one another. After the sender is finished and the receiver has mirrored, validated, and empathized, the couple switches roles. Sender becomes receiver and receiver becomes sender, still on the same topic, so as not to stack up issues, allowing both partners' realities to exist on the one topic.

Mike and I first learned couples dialogue at a weekend workshop that I had to attend to become an Imago therapist. I recall thinking, *If Mike and I are in such bad shape that we have to talk like this for the rest of our lives, then it's not worth it.* It felt tedious and mechanical. And it is. But, after practicing it for a while, we realized that it helped us to hear each other more accurately and deeply. Now we use it only if we're too reactive. It's saved us from a lot of fights that, before, would have left both of us with hurt feelings.

If you want to speak to your partner, make an appointment. Sounds trite, but it works. The partner who has a frustration tells the other what's going on. "Is this is a good time to discuss it?" If the other partner says no, the two negotiate for a better time. We recommend that couples not wait more than 24 hours.

After the Power Struggle

Once couples move through the power struggle stage, then they can commit even more deeply. Here are some ways to accomplish this:

What do you call your man? *Lover* was most commonly used until the 1990s. During the 1990s, we've seen a shift from "lover" to "partner." In her book, *Permanent Partners*, Betty Berzon, attributes this shift to the legalization of live-together relationships.[5] Gays and lesbians began to realize the need to protect themselves and their partners legally, but the word "lover" was inappropriate in legal documents. Thus "partner" became more widely used.

As a gay man, I wear a wedding ring and expect my husband to be invited to all events I'm invited to. And I enjoy talking about Mike to others. Society may tell me that I'm pushing my relationship into people's faces, when all I've ever wanted are the very same rights, privileges, and recognition my sister and her spouse enjoy. Legally married, she wears her wedding band, talks openly about her husband, and brings him to all special events and family gatherings. No one would think of saying to her, "Honey, we don't want to hear about your sex life. So take off that wedding band. Don't talk about your husband. And don't expect to bring him around, because we don't want to see him. You're just shoving your sexuality down our throats."

I want to publicly celebrate my love for Mike. And I want to share in Mike's insurance benefits. If he dies before I do, I won't receive any of his Social Security benefits, as a legal widow would. I want to help make decisions should Mike fall ill or be injured. But as a "single" person, not legally bound to him, I have none of these rights. A hospital could deny me entry to his room because I'm not legally part of his family. He and I have taken care of this in our wills and have legal power of attorney for each other, so I could go to court to prove our agreement —but what a hassle. Worries like that cause stress in a relationship.

Both in and outside my practice, I'm often shocked to meet gay couples who've been together for a number of years, who share a home and expenses, yet still refer to themselves as boyfriends. To me, a *boyfriend* is someone you date. Using words like "friend" or "boyfriend" minimizes the level of your commitment and throws up a barrier to deeper levels of intimacy.

Whether you're straight or gay, it's always easier to decide not to commit more deeply. For one thing, being noncommittal allows you a handy, guilt-free exit: "Well, if this doesn't work out, I can always leave. This relationship isn't like a real marriage, so I don't have to abide by any rules." Marriage helps couples achieve a psychological intimacy they might not otherwise experience. First of all, merely considering marriage promotes a deeper commitment between the two partners. Deciding to go for it prompts all kinds of new hopes, questions, and insecurities.

By committing more fully to a male partner and thereby becoming more visible and "out," you'll face hurdles you'd never encounter if you were straight. Heterosexual brides and their fiancés are usually overwhelmed by the demands of their respective families. If anyone asked them, "Does your wedding have a political agenda?" they'd be surprised at such a ridiculous question. For gays and lesbians, however, just the idea of having a wedding is politically loaded. I've heard many gay men use this as the reason not to have a ceremony. I believe that rationale is often just another exit—a way of avoiding a deeper commitment to oneself and to one's partner.

Marriage

Marriage isn't for everyone, but Gottman's research shows that heterosexual couples who simply live together (or "cohabitate") are more likely to break up than couples who commit more deeply. Again our deepest healing as individuals—and especially as gay men—is achieved in a committed adult love relationship.

When I say "marriage," I hasten to add that I don't care what you call your ceremony. Use whatever works for you. For the sake of this discussion, I'll just use "marriage," since that's what works for me. The idea is to have a ceremony with the elements and overtones of a wedding.

Planning a marriage will recall your earlier romantic times, but also deepen your power struggle, because you're tightening the space between the two of you. The experience will stir events from childhood, when you first encountered this type of relational closeness. The type of family you grew up in will determine how you react to the new dynamics in your current relationship.

When Larry and Curt first met they fell madly in love— romantic love, that is. Larry adored Curt's assertiveness and found him to be a very passionate man. Curt loved Larry's independence. They enjoyed a wonderful year of togetherness. When they agreed to live together, they decided to go all the way and get married. As they moved forward with their wedding plans, Larry began to see Curt's assertiveness as domineering. And to Curt, Larry's independence began to feel like lack of interest.

During therapy with me, they discovered something that surprised them both. Larry had been raised by a dominant, authoritarian father who was extremely rule-oriented and who demanded things go his way. Suddenly Larry began to perceive these same traits in Curt. Yes, Curt was passionate about things he wanted for the wedding, but he wasn't being domineering. Yet Larry took it that way—clearly a projection we needed to work through in therapy.

Curt was raised by an uninvolved mother who neglected him through most of his childhood. He was better at planning and had more ideas for the wedding; therefore Larry tended to defer to him. But instead of seeing Larry's easygoing cooperation for what it was, Curt felt that he was being ignored and left to his own devices. He too was regressing to childhood. As you'll recall from Chapter 9, this kind of power struggle is supposed to happen and is a positive indicator of a healthy relationship. But while it's happening, it's not much fun.

Mike and I ran into similar challenges in planning our wedding. First, what were we going to call our upcoming celebration? Some gays and lesbians call it a commitment ceremony, others call it a union. We were a couple of traditional guys; for us, the words "wedding" and "marriage" seemed most apt.

Since both of us are men, we knew nothing about planning a wedding. Women (especially the mother of the bride) tend to be the driving force behind weddings. They talk to their girlfriends, sisters, and mothers and support one another in the planning. Magazines typically focus on the bride, as does the language of marriage: *bridal* showers, *bridal* party, *bridal* gown. We resolved that problem by hiring a party planner to take care of all the details. This also reduced the amount of conflict between us and our families in handling the wedding plans by having a third party involved. And thankfully, it worked!

Next, we had to decide where to hold the wedding. Thankfully, Reform Judaism recognizes gay marriages, and I am a Reform Jew. Our wonderful rabbi agreed to perform the ceremony.

We considered ourselves engaged and decided to publicly declare our engagement in print, as other couples do. So we sent our picture and announcement to a local newspaper, who returned them with the reply, "We are not ready for this right now."

Though this hurt us deeply, Mike and I didn't allow this setback to stop us. Our next step was to select a gay-friendly photographer, videographer, florist, and band. Our party planner assumed the risk of facing homophobia in his search. And sure enough, he did. I told him to assure prospective candidates that ours would be a traditional, conservative wedding where nothing "unusual" would occur.

Because many people equate "gay" with sex, their minds focus only on that aspect of our lives. Our planner reported he'd had the most problems with musicians who were concerned about witnessing the "emotion between two men." We realized this isn't really a gay issue: The society we live in simply doesn't honor or support affection between men in general. Even with limited choices, our planner helped us find an excellent band.

Instead of tossing the bouquet and garter belt (neither of which figured into our plans), we decided to throw Bert and Ernie from *Sesame Street*. A few years before our wedding, some organizations had "outed" them as a gay couple. ("They take baths together and sleep in the same bed together; this is modeling homosexuality.") We honored Bert and Ernie as a fine "gay couple" and asked our florist to create table settings using small Bert and Ernie puppets and a Tinky Winky doll, all tied together in a bow with a tag honoring them as "A Perfect Family."

Registering for our gifts required a few changes, as did the marriage contract. We laughed when the forms asked for the names of bride and groom. Whoever filled it out made the other partner the bride. Though we did have some fun with this, it did seem sad that wedding jargon makes no room for gay couples. Someday, we hope, there'll be options for grooms and grooms, and brides and brides.

Next came the bachelor parties. Because we're both men, we had one party for us both. The wife of one straight male friend had banned him from bachelor parties, because he had gotten into trouble in the past—but she had no qualms about his attending a gay male bachelor party.

Everything else went smoothly. Mike and I were married under a traditional *chuppah,* or wedding canopy, supported by four firm poles over the *beama,* or altar, where synagogue weddings take place. Our family and friends were all there and we felt loved and supported. We wanted to be open about our love and commitment. We wanted a place at the table—and we took it for ourselves.

There's a great song by Fred Small, "Everything Possible." It used to be sung by a LGBTQ group called The Flirtations, who are no longer together. I use it at the end of the workshops and, because I think the song applies to us all, I'm including here in its entirety:

We have cleared off the table, the leftovers saved
Washed the dishes and put them away
I have told you a story and tucked you in tight
At the end of your knockabout day
As the moon sets its sails to carry you to sleep
Over the midnight sea
I will sing you a song no one sang to me
May it keep you good company

You can be anybody you want to be
You can love whomever you will
You can travel any country where your heart leads
And know I will love you still
You can live by yourself, you can gather friends around
You can choose one special one
And the only measure of your words and your deeds
Will be the love you leave behind when you're done

There are girls who grow up strong and bold
There are boys quiet and kind
Some race on ahead, some follow behind
Some go in their own way and time
Some women love women, some men love men

Some raise children, some never do
You can dream all the day never reaching the end
Of everything possible for you

Don't be rattled by names, by taunts, by games
But seek out spirits true
If you give your friends the best part of yourself
They will give the same back to you[6]

References

1. www.gottman.com.
2. Mubarak Dahir. "A Gay Thing," in *The Windy City Times*, February 21, 2001.
3. www.gottman.com. "What Makes Same-Sex Relationships Succeed or Fail."
4. Harville Hendrix. *Getting The Love You Want: A Guide for Couples*. New York: Henry Holt & Co., 1988.
5. Betty Berzon. *Permanent Partners: Building Gay and Lesbian Relationships That Last*. New York: Penguin Books, 1988.
6. Copyright 1983 by Fred Small. Used by permission. All rights reserved.

Bibliography

1. Bob Bergeron. *Right Side of Forty: The Complete Guide to Happiness for Gay Men at Midlife and Beyond.* New York: Magnus Books, 2012.
2. Betty Berzon. *Permanent Partners: Building Gay and Lesbian Relationships That Last.* New York: Penguin Books, 1988.
3. Robert Bly. *A Little Book on the Human Shadow.* New York: HarperCollins Publishers, 1988.
4. Douglas Braun-Harvey and Michael Vigorito. *Treating Out of Control Sexual Behavior: Rethinking Sex Addiction.* New York: Springer, 2015.
5. Vivienne Cass. "Homosexual Identity Formation: A Theoretical Model," in *Journal of Homosexuality*, Vol. 4 (3), 1979, 219-235.
6. Center for Disease Control and Prevention, "Sexually Transmitted Diseases (STDs)," www.cdc.gov/std/
7. Susan A. Clancy. *The Trauma Myth: The Truth About the Sexual Abuse of Children—and Its Aftermath.* New York: Basic Books, 2011.
8. Mubarak Dahir. "A Gay Thing," in *The Windy City Times*, February 21, 2001.
9. Tina Dupuy, "Legalized: Oral Sex, Sodomy and Immoral Prosecutions," Huffington Post, 09/21/2009, updated 5/25/2011.
10. Dianne Elise. "Tomboys and Cowgirls: The Girl's Disidentification from the Mother" in *Sissies and Tomboys: Gender Nonconformity and Homosexual Childhood,* Matthew Rottnek, ed. New York University Press, 1999, 140-152.
11. Erik Erikson. *Childhood and Society.* New York: W.W. Norton and Company, 1963.

12. Erik H. Erikson and Joan M. Erikson. *The Life Cycle Completed* extended version. New York: W. W. Norton & Company, 1998.

13. Helen Fisher. *Anatomy of Love: A Natural History of Mating, Marriage, and Why We Stray*, revised edition. New York: W. W. Norton & Company, 2016.

14. John and Julie Gottman, "What Makes Same-Sex Relationships Succeed or Fail," The Gottman Institute, www.gottman.com.

15. Richard Green. *The "Sissy Boy Syndrome" and the Development of Homosexuality*. New Haven: Yale University Press, 1987.

16. Harville Hendrix. *Getting The Love You Want: A Guide for Couples*. New York: Henry Holt and Company, 1988.

17. Harville Hendrix, Ph.D. *Keeping the Love You Find: A Guide for Singles*. New York: Owl Books; Reprint edition, 2001.

18. Richard Isay. *Being Homosexual: Gay Men and Their Development*. The Master Work Series, Softcover Edition, New Jersey: Jason Aronson, 1994.

19. Richard Isay. *Becoming Gay: The Journey to Self-Acceptance*. New York: Pantheon Books, 1996.

20. Michael E. Kerr and Murray Bowen. *Family Evaluation: An Approach Based on Bowen Theory*. Toronto: Penguin Books, Canada, 1988.

21. Sharon Kleinberg and Patricia Zorn. "Multiple Mirroring with Lesbian and Gay Couples: From Peoria to P-Town," in *Healing in the Relational Paradigm: The Imago Relationship Therapy Casebook*, edited by Wade Luquet and Mo Therese Hannah. Second edition. Washington, D.C.: Brunner-Routledge, 1998.

22. Maya Kollman. "Helping Couples Get the Love They Want," *In The Family* magazine, April, 1997.

23. Harold Kooden with Charles Flowers. *Golden Men: The Power of Gay Midlife*. New York: Avon Books, 2000.

24. Joe Kort. *10 Smart Things Gay Men Can Do to Find Real Love*. New York: Alyson Books, 2003.

25. Joe Kort. *Gay Affirmative Therapy for the Straight Clinician: The Essential Guide*. New York: W. W. Norton & Company, 2008.
26. Joe Kort. "Guys on the 'Side': Looking Beyond Gay Tops and Bottoms," *Huffington Post*, April 16, 2013.
27. Joe Kort with Alexander Morgan. *Is My Husband Gay, Straight, or Bi?: A Guide for Women Concerned about Their Men*. Lanham, Maryland: Rowman & Littlefield Publishers, 2014.
28. Michael C. LaSala. "Monogamous or Not: Understanding and Counseling Gay Male Couples," *Families in Society*, Vol. 82 (6), 2000.
29. Brian McNaught. *On Being Gay: Thoughts on Family, Faith, and Love*. New York: St. Martin's Press, 1983.
30. Brian McNaught. *Gay Issues in the Workplace*. New York: St. Martin's Press, 1993.
31. Brian McNaught. *Now That I'm Out, What Do I Do?* New York: St. Martin's Press, 1997.
32. Alice Miller. *The Drama of the Gifted Child: The Search for the True Self*. New York: Basic Books, 1981.
33. Jack Morin. *The Erotic Mind: Unlocking the Inner Sources of Sexual Passion and Fulfillment*. Harper Perennial, 1996.
34. Esther Perel, "The Secret to Desire in a Long-term Relationship," TED talk, posted Feb 2013.
35. John R. Stowe. *Gay Spirit Warrior: An Empowerment Workbook for Men Who Love Men*. Tallahassee, Florida: Findhorn Press, 1999.
36. Andrew Tobias (first published under the pseudonym John Reid), *The Best Little Boy in the World*, 25th Anniversary Edition. New York: Ballantine Books, 1993.
37. Tristan Taormino. *Opening Up: A Guide to Creating and Sustaining Open Relationships*. Berkeley, California: Cleis Press, 2008.
38. Anastasia Toufexis. "The Right Chemistry," *Time*, June 24, 2001.

Acknowledgments

This book is dedicated to Mike Cramer, my husband, with whom I've lived and learned these Ten Things, and whose love and patience sustained me throughout. You have taught me about integrity, trust, and commitment. You have taught me what family really means. You make the world safe for me.

To Jim Gerardi, who encouraged me to write the book and got me started on it.

I want to express special thanks to my beloved sister Lisa Kort-Jaisinghani and her family, especially my nephews and niece—Jacob, Zachary, Noah, and Zoe—whose sweet presence in my life is such a blessing.

To Barb Shumard, MSW, whose supervision and guidance allowed me to mature and grow as a therapist and to help the clients who seek my services.

To Lynn Grodzki, MSW, whose coaching and teaching laid the groundwork that made it possible for me to write this book.

I'm especially grateful to all the gay men and gay couples whose courageous work I have been privileged to witness. I have been honored to be a part of your lives and to help you grow into the fine gay men who now surround me in the gay community. I have learned a great deal from you. Thank you.

I want to acknowledge my mother-in-law, Lee Cramer, who is not here to read my completed work and who was one of my biggest champions when I decided to write this book.

I want to thank my writer and editor Alexander Morgan, without whom I could not have revised this book so eloquently. Alex took a fine tooth comb and went over every chapter with me, ensuring that the book spoke to the gay men of today. I am very grateful for the time and energy he put into this with me.

Made in the USA
Lexington, KY
02 September 2016